AF469136

Author

Anne Bouji

Published by:

Al Roya Press & Publishing House
P.O. Box 343, Postal Code 118, Muscat, Sultanate of Oman
Tel: (968) 24479888, Fax: (968) 24479889
E-mail: alroya@omantel.net.om www.alroya.net

This is

Oman

Al Roya Press and Publishing House
P.O. Box 343, Postal Code 118, Al Harthy Complex, Muscat, Sultanate of Oman
Tel: (968) 24479888, Fax: (968) 24479889
E-mail: alroya@omantel.net.om www.alroya.net

Publisher
Hatim Al Taie

Author
Anne Bouji

Design and Production
Dhian Chand

Photography by
Arthur Thevenart
Hanne & Jens Eriksen
Shakeel Al Balushi
Tony Walsh

Printed by
Modern Colour Printers

First Published October 2003
New edition November 2011

ISBN : 978 9948 1625 06
Registration No: 295/2011

SULTANATE OF OMAN

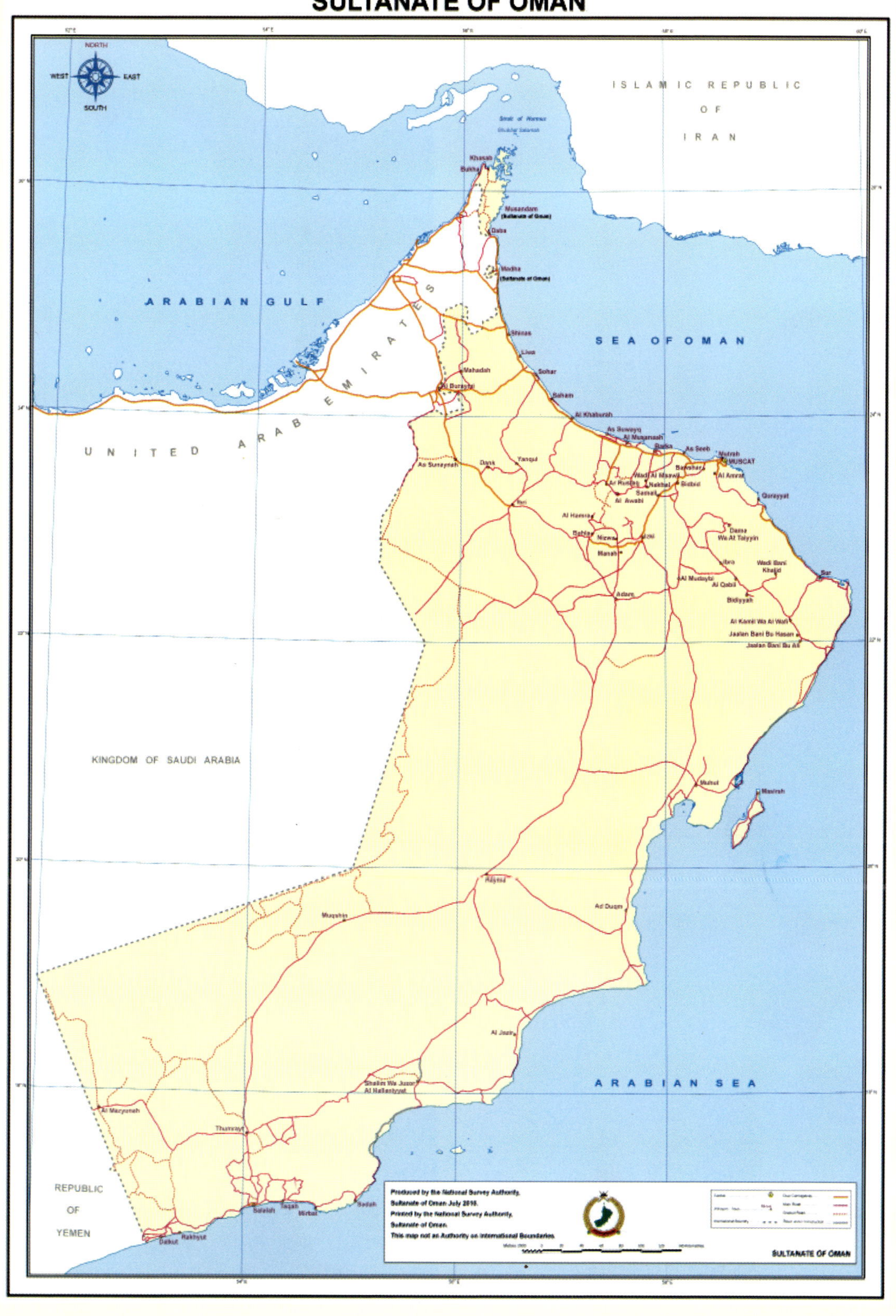

DAWN OVER OMAN

His Majesty's first address to the nation;

"I promise you to proceed forthwith in the process of creating a modern government. My first act will be the immediate abolition of all the unnecessary restrictions on your lives and activities.

My people, I will proceed as quickly as possible to transform your life into a prosperous one with a bright future. Every one of you must play his part towards this goal. Our country in the past was famous and strong. If we work in unity and cooperation we will regenerate that glorious past and we will take a respectable place in the world.

I call upon you to continue living as usual. I will be arriving in Muscat in the coming days and then I will let you know of my future plans.

My people, I and my new government will work to achieve our general objective.

My people, my brothers, yesterday it was complete darkness and with the help of God, tomorrow will be a new dawn on Muscat, Oman and its people.

God bless us all and may He grant our efforts success."

And so began the reign of Sultan Qaboos on 23 July 1970.

CONTENTS

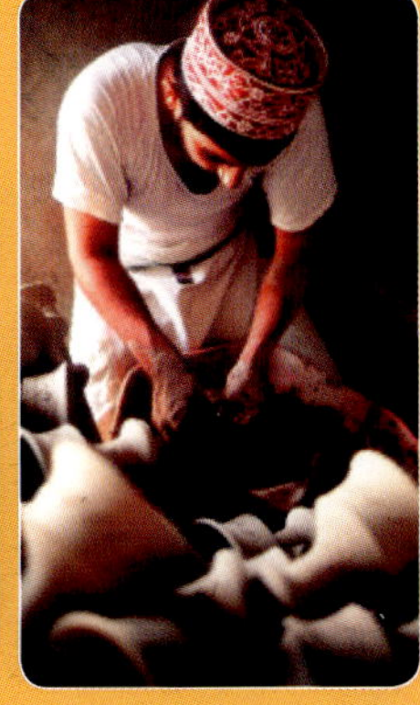

Part I

Culture & Tradition — Pages 12-105

Part II

Regions & Fables — Pages 106-180

CULTURE & TRADITION

List of Contents

What is an Arab? 12
Islam 14
Ancient History 16
H.M. Sultan Qaboos 18
Modern History 20
Coffee, Dates & Hospitality 24
Henna 26
Khanjar 28
National Costumes 30
Currency & Postage Stamps 34
Dhows. 36
The Falaj 40
Omani Flag 41
Forts 42
Frankincense and Myrrh 44
Mosques 50
Silver & Gold 52
Souqs 54
Camels 57
Fish & Marine Life 61
Turtles 64
Wildlife 65
Horses and Equestrian Sports 74
Caves in Oman 78
UNESCO sites in Oman 81
Rocks and Minerals 86
Oman's Healing Springs 90
Royal Botanic Gardens 92
Oman's Museums 94
Oman in the Guinness Book of Records 102

What is an Arab?

Many people find it difficult to distinguish between the Muslim world, the Arab world, the Middle East and the Gulf States.

The Muslim world includes any part of the world where Islam is the main religion. This, therefore, includes parts of North Africa, Somalia, Pakistan, Turkey, Iraq, Iran, Afghanistan and Indonesia.

Russia and China have large Muslim populations but are not classed as Muslim countries. There are 1.6 billion Muslims in the world which is 23 % of the world's population. There are more Muslims in Germany than in Lebanon and China has a larger Muslim population than Syria. Indonesia has the world's largest Muslim population.

The Arab World is made up of 21 countries with 280 million people and encompasses Western Asia and North Africa. It is those nations that have Arabic as their main language but may also have religions other than Islam as their national religion. These include the nations of North Africa, where most people will speak and read Arabic, but also have other groups living there too. In Oman, languages other than Arabic are spoken, such as Swahili, Balushi, Lutiani and English, but Arabic is the official language.

The Middle East encompasses Western Asia and North Africa and is home to many ethnic groups including Arabs, Turks, Persians, Jews, Kurds, Armenians, Greeks and many more. The Middle East is the centre of the Arab World. The word Arab actually means nomad and the original Arabs came from Yemen in the south western part of the Arabian Peninsula. Arabs are descended from two main tribes, the Qahtan in Southern Arabian peninsula and the Northern Arabians from Adnan. As Islam spread from Medina and Mecca in what is now Saudi Arabia, the Arabic language spread with it. The Middle East is approximately two thirds of the size of the United States of America and twenty-five times bigger than Britain. Much of the area is empty because of the vast desert regions and harsh conditions. Saudi Arabia is nine times bigger than Britain, but has roughly the same population as London.

Parts of the Middle East are amongst the hottest and driest in the world and temperatures can reach over fifty degrees centigrade during the day, though in the desert at night it can be cold and in areas of Iran and Lebanon it snows in the winter. The Middle East separates Europe and Africa from Asia and has played an important role in world trade – even before oil was discovered. Oil may have been produced for industrial use in Saudi Arabia since 1938, but Arabs have been using oil for two hundred years to treat leather and for boat building.

Arabic is the language of the Holy Quran and Islam. From simple beginnings in the desert, it spread and developed into a vast Islamic empire. As long ago as the 8th century, doctors, poets, artists and architects flourished and the language became more complex to cope with new discoveries.

Western scholars owe a great debt to Arab scholars as they have used many Arab inventions. Perhaps the most widely used is that of coffee. It was an Arab who first boiled berries to drink and thus coffee was born and quickly spread to the rest of the world. The first pin hole camera was invented by an Arab, a10th-century Muslim mathematician, astronomer and physicist Ibn al-Haitham. A thousand years before the Wright brothers a Muslim poet, astronomer, musician and engineer named Abbas Ibn Firnas made several attempts to construct a flying machine. In 852 he jumped from the minaret of the Grand Mosque in Cordoba using a loose cloak stiffened with wooden struts. He hoped to glide like a bird, but did not. However the cloak slowed his fall, creating what is thought to be the first parachute. Washing and bathing are religious requirements for Muslims, which is perhaps why they perfected the recipe for soap which we still use today.

Written Arabic is read from right to left. There are twenty-eight letters in the alphabet, which are all consonants; vowels are added by using dots or small lines. Some Arabic numbers look similar to those we use in the western world and, in fact, English numbers are actually called Arabic numerals because they originated from Arabic.

The Gulf States are those States that make up the Arabian Peninsula and are the Kingdom of Saudi Arabia, The United Arab Emirates, Qatar, Bahrain, Kuwait and the Sultanate of Oman. The Gulf States are some of the richest countries in the world.

Oman is therefore part of the Arabian Gulf, the Arab World, the Middle East and the Muslim World.

Islam

Oman embraced Islam *circa* 628-630 AD.
Islam had been spreading throughout the Arab lands when the Prophet sent his messenger to the two Kings of Oman, Jaifar and Abd. Oman embraced Islam voluntarily and then played a major role in the spread of Islam into Basra in the south of Iraq, East Africa and China.

Mazin bin Ghadouba was the first Omani to go to Mecca in Saudi Arabia, where he met the Prophet Mohammed and became the first Omani Muslim. Most Omanis belong to the Ibadi Muslim faith, but there are also some Shia and some Sunni Muslims. They all live in harmony and respect each other's beliefs. The Ibadis believe that the Imam is their spiritual and political leader. Al Julanda bin Masud was the first publicly elected Imam of the Ibadi faith in Oman.

Some of the basic principles of Islam.

Islam is much more than a religion; it is a way of life, a code of living standards and the basis of the law. Prayer is very important to Muslims who pray five times a day. Most people think that Muslims pray facing the east, but it is more accurate to say that Muslims pray facing the Holy City of Mecca, so in Oman this means that Muslims pray facing northwest. No Muslim will pray or enter a mosque unclean, so there is a traditional washing ceremony that must be performed before beginning to pray. Only then will a Muslim present himself before God, entering the mosque without socks and shoes and stepping forward with his right leg.

A Muslim will not eat pork, drink alcohol, gamble, tell lies or eat the meat of any animal that is already dead. All meat that is to be eaten is killed in the *Halal* tradition so that all blood is drained from the animal. A Muslim will not eat using his left hand. In the Holy month of Ramadan, all Muslims who are able to do so will not eat, drink or smoke in the hours from sunrise to sunset. When entering a room a Muslim will greet those people already in the room. A Muslim who is walking will greet those who are seated. A Muslim who is riding will greet those who are walking and an individual will always greet a group.

The five pillars of Islam observed by all Muslims are:

1. Believe in God and profess that there is no other God but Allah. Believe in his angels, his messengers, afterlife, fate and destiny.
2. Pray five times a day facing Mecca.
3. Fast during the Holy Month of Ramadan.
4. Help the poor and needy- Zakat.
5. If possible Muslims should go on a pilgrimage to Mecca at least once in their lifetime to perform the Hajj.

Oman's Ancient History

Archaeology has proved that there has been civilization in Oman for five thousand years. Ancient manuscripts record events and trade with Magan (the name given to Oman by the Sumerians and the Mesopotamians *circa* 3000 BC, and Mazoun the name used by the Persians. Magan, probably refers to the copper mines and trade in copper, and Mazoun to the abundance of water that has made farming possible in some areas.

Oman may come from the Yemeni name Uman, which is where some of the tribes migrated from to settle in Oman. Tribes from many different countries have settled in Oman over the years.

In the early 16th century, the Portuguese invaded Oman and captured Muscat, where they stayed for a hundred and fifty years. Imam Nasser bin Murshid and his successor Saif bin Sultan Al Ya'arubi defeated the Portuguese and expelled them from the country. In the course of the Ya'aruba dynasty, Oman prospered and many of the historic buildings and forts date back to that time.

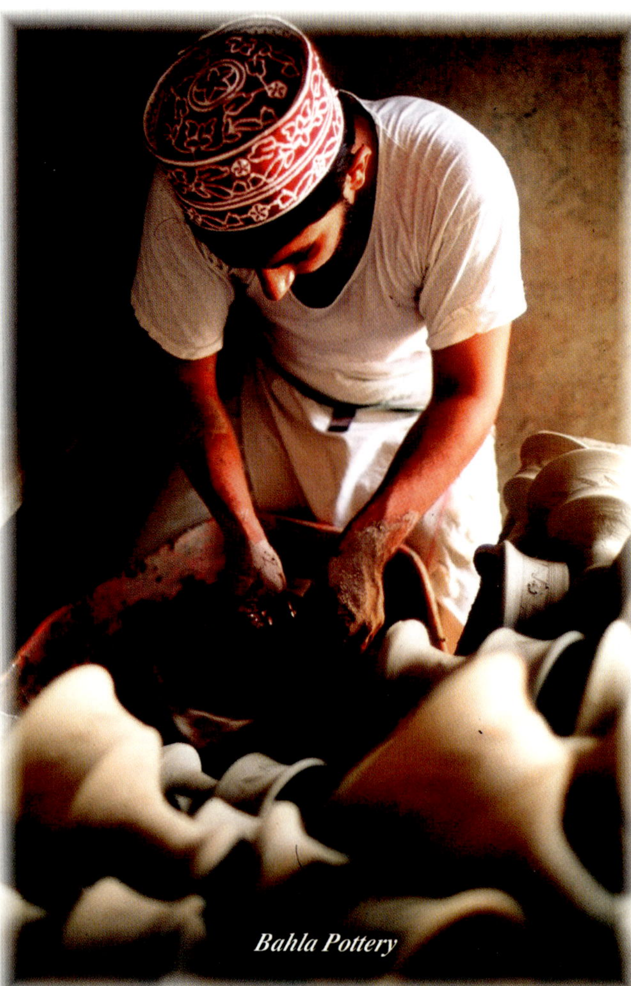

Bahla Pottery

A civil war caused the tribes to elect a new Imam and the Persians used this opportunity to invade Oman. Unity was restored to the country when the Persians were expelled by the Al Busaidi dynasty in 1744. Since this time no foreign power has invaded Oman.

Oman prospered, built a strong navy and merchant fleet and created an empire that included

East Africa and both sides of the Gulf. Zanzibar was named as the second capital of Oman in 1832. By the middle of the 19th century, Oman dominated trade around the Indian Ocean.

Political links were established with France, Britain and the USA. In 1840 the first diplomatic envoy was sent to the United States and was headed by Ahmed Bin Nu'man Al Ka'abi. He sailed from Zanzibar on the '*Sultana*,' which means Princess, to New York.

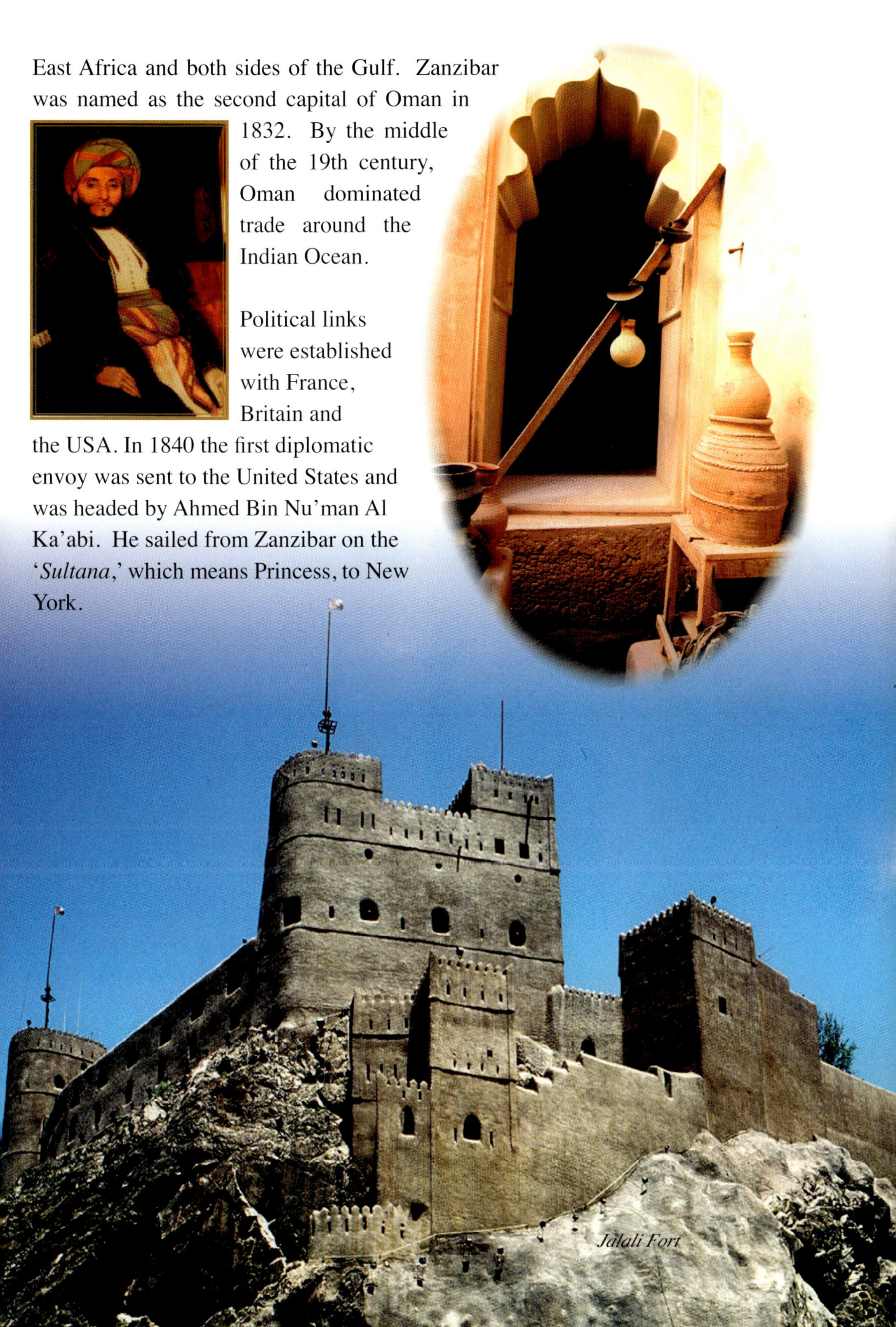

Jalali Fort

His Majesty Sultan Qaboos bin Said Al Said

His Majesty Sultan Qaboos was born in Salalah, the most southerly city of the state then known as Muscat and Oman, on 18th November 1940. He was the only son of the late Sultan Said bin Taimur and the eighth direct descendant of the royal Al Busaidi line founded in 1744 by Imam Ahmad bin Said. Sultan Qaboos spent his childhood in Salalah. When he reached the age of 16, his father sent him to a private school in England, and in 1960 he entered The Royal Military Academy Sandhurst as an officer cadet.

After passing out from Sandhurst, he spent a year with a British infantry battalion on duty in Germany and then held a staff appointment with the British army. Later, speaking to young officers at a passing out parade, Sultan Qaboos recalled his own military training. *"The values that I absorbed have remained with me forever afterwards,"* he said. "*I learned that discipline is not just something one imposes on others; it is something that one has, above all, to apply to oneself, if one is to be a worthy leader of men. I also learned the true meaning of service: that is, to give, and not to expect to receive, and that it is the team, and not oneself, that matters. I learned that with responsibility comes obligation."*

Having finished his military service, His Majesty studied local government in England and then embarked on a tour of the world. When he returned to Oman in 1964, the following six years were spent studying Islam and Omani history in Salalah. On the abdication of his father and his subsequent accession on 23rd July

1970, Sultan Qaboos moved to Muscat to implement his vision for the country's development.

Like his famous ancestor Imam Ahmad, the founder of the Al Busaidi dynasty, an outstanding leader who had ended a turbulent era of civil wars and brought peace and stability to Oman, Sultan Qaboos inherited a stagnant, conflict-ridden country. In his first address to the nation, he declared that the country would be unified as the Sultanate of Oman, with a new flag, and ended restrictions on freedom of movement. He called on Omanis who had left the country to return home in order to contribute to the challenges that lay ahead and to use their talents and expertise to modernise a once powerful nation that had fallen into poverty and decline.

Apart from his role as ruler, His Majesty Sultan Qaboos is a man of diverse interests. He has been an enthusiastic horseman since childhood and enjoys other outdoor pursuits, including walking and tennis. His military training has left him with a keen interest in weapons and military equipment; he is an adept marksman and is proud of the Omani shooting team's numerous international successes. He has studied a variety of subjects ranging from religion to astronomy and the environment, languages, literature and history. His passion for music led him to establish the Royal Oman Symphony Orchestra in 1985.

Modern History

The recent history of Oman is as interesting and fascinating as the ancient history due to the leadership and support of His Majesty Sultan Qaboos.

By 1970, most people in the western world were watching colour TV and had automatic washing machines in their homes. They thought nothing of getting on an aeroplane to fly to the furthest corners of the world for a summer vacation. America had successfully landed Neil Armstrong on the moon, to take that one small step for mankind, but in Oman, things were very different.

There was a curfew from sunset to sunrise each day, when the city gates in Muscat were closed and locked. If you wanted to go out after dark you had to carry a kerosene lantern and not a torch. The reason for this was that a torch throws a beam of light away from the person carrying it and a lantern throws its light upon the person carrying it. When the guards stopped people who were out after sunset to ask if they were friend or foe, the lantern helped the guards to identify people. Sunglasses and radios were not allowed and there were no newspapers.

In 1970 there were only 3 government primary schools in Oman, and these were for boys only. There were only 10 kilometers of sealed road and 1 hospital with just 12 beds.

Today there are more than 1000 Government schools providing full time education, free of cost to both boys and girls. Almost 45,000 male and female teachers are employed to teach the nation's 543,000 children and 713 children in special needs places, so that every Omani can have the advantage of the gifts and opportunities that Education brings. An additional 100,000 pupils attend one of the 350 private schools in the Sultanate. Oman can now boast a number of higher education colleges, technical and vocational training institutes and the Sultan Qaboos University which currently has 15,200 students. SQU began in 1986 with just 5 colleges and offered only bachelor's degrees. Today more than, 2700 students enrolled for courses this academic year in a university that now offers masters' and doctorate degrees from 9 colleges. There are also a number of private universities affiliated to universities in the UK and USA. 40 countries worldwide host a total of over 31,000 Omani students who are studying abroad.

Thanks to His Majesty's planning and concern for the welfare of his people there are now 60 hospitals and 242 health centres as with a total of 5,600 beds. In addition there are a growing number of private hospitals clinics and laboratories. Oman's Ministry of Health provides 3,900 doctors, almost 10,000 nurses, 240 pharmacists and 231 dentists.

Since 1970, ten kilometers of sealed road have grown to almost 126,000 kilometers.

There is a major 1000 kilometer highway between Muscat and Salalah, and a sophisticated road network covering the whole of the country. In the Sultan's 40th year of his reign, a superhighway, the Muscat Expressway was opened linking the Qurum area of the capital to Sohar and major roads to the south of the country. This tremendous feat of engineering is currently 54 kms in length with numerous bridges, underpasses and interchanges. This has enabled traffic to flow more freely and will hopefully help to reduce accidents, enhance delivery services and will support tourism.

There are now major seaports and international airports. Tourism is an important feature generating employment and income for the country.

Oman radio began broadcasting in July 1970 and television began in September 1974. Oman was one of the first countries in the Gulf States to use a satellite for domestic transmission, and in 1996 Oman established a website, Omannet, to promote official information about the country. There are currently approximately 180,000 subscribers who have internet access. The media has grown tremendously in the 40 years since His Majesty came to power. Oman now has private radio and TV stations. There are a host of magazines and free circulation newspapers and magazines. There are at least 20 printing houses with a large number of presses

Sultan Qaboos Universty

in the private sector, advertising agencies and media distributors. Oman now has 9 daily newspapers.

All of this, and much more, in just 40 years! Oman has developed into a united country, progressive and modern, but still maintaining its cultural and Islamic traditions.

In 2011 many reforms have taken place in Oman and His Majesty keen to ensure the safety, security and welfare of his people and his country has introduced a number of changes and issued royal degrees to help Oman cope with developments in the region and the world at large.

Oman has a land mass of 309,500 square kilometers, and a national population in of 1,957,336 Omanis and 816,143 expatriates.(*figs. as per the National Census of Dec. 2010)*

Coffee, Dates & Hospitality

In Oman and most of the Arab world, the coffee pot is the sign of hospitality. It is so important that there are a number of roadside ornaments depicting the traditional coffee pot at the side of the main highway.

In Oman, local coffee is called *Kawah.* This is a blend of coffee sometimes to which cardamom is added to enhance the flavour and is served in tiny cups without handles called *finjan.* The cup is shaken from side to side to indicate that you have enjoyed the hospitality but do not want any more coffee.

Kawah is offered to all visitors in Government offices, some small village shops and in most Omani homes. When visiting an Omani home, *kawah* will often be served with dates.

Dates are an integral part of life in Oman and many other Arabian countries. The seeds of dates are often used as coffee beans, especially by the Bedouin. The date palm provides food of the highest nutritional value, and the palm fronds can be woven into matting, used as walls for temporary housing for the Bedouin or as fencing for goats and sheep, shaped into baskets and even made into *barasti* boats.

Dates, which may be eaten fresh or sun dried, have a very high nutritional value and are low in fat. They provide protein, natural sugar, essential minerals and vitamins, and are very high in fibre. They are often used to

feed racing camels, which need abundant sources of energy. The Bedouin people of the desert regions can survive on goat's milk or camel's milk and dates for a very long time. There are 200 varieties of dates grown in Oman. In the holy month of Ramadan, many people use dates to break their fast, because of their nutritional value. Dates also feature in weddings, festivals and celebrations. Dates have been exported from Oman for many hundreds of years, and are shipped to the USA, East Africa, India and other countries. When Oman was a major seafaring nation, the capacity of a ship was measured by the number of sacks of dates that it could carry.

Henna

Henna art is as important as jewellery and make-up, to an Omani woman. For weddings, religious festivals, holidays and sometimes just for fun, Omani women and young girls decorate their hands and feet with henna.

Henna is made by extracting a dye from a local plant, called *Lawsonia Inermis,* and though this plant has small, perfumed white flowers, it is the leaves that provide the dye. Henna powder is mixed with sun-dried limes and is painted onto the skin in delicate and often very intricate patterns. The henna is allowed to dry and when rubbed off, leaves behind a dark brown stain which fades over a period of time. To make the colour ever darker, a mixture of lemon juice and sugar can be applied on top of the henna and then left to dry. On some occasions men too will have the tips of their fingers, their feet or even their whole hand dipped into henna to provide a uniform stain, without the pattern.

A hand decorated with henna

Henna is also used as a hair dye and in traditional medicine to relieve headaches or reduce high temperatures. For a bride, the henna ceremony is one of the most important aspects of the wedding preparations when the bride's female relatives and friends gather together to prepare her for her wedding day. On these occasions there is much singing and dancing. The bride of course cannot take part in any of the festivities as she is unable to move or she would spoil the patterns of the henna.

Khanjar

The *Khanjar* is a curved dagger worn by Omani men on ceremonial, cultural and other special occasions, though it was originally worn for protection. Traditional *khanjars* are made of silver, but there are some made of gold.

The curved dagger has a flat-topped handle and is kept in a curved wooden holder which is covered with leather and decorated with silver thread woven into intricate patterns. The handle was originally made of rhino horn, but is now made of plastic or bone. The handle is decorated with beaten silver and silver threads. The *khanjar* is worn attached to a belt, which is also decorated with silver threads and is attached to the belt with silver rings.

The best quality *khanjar* has seven silver rings. Some *khanjars* have a small pouch attached to the back of the cover

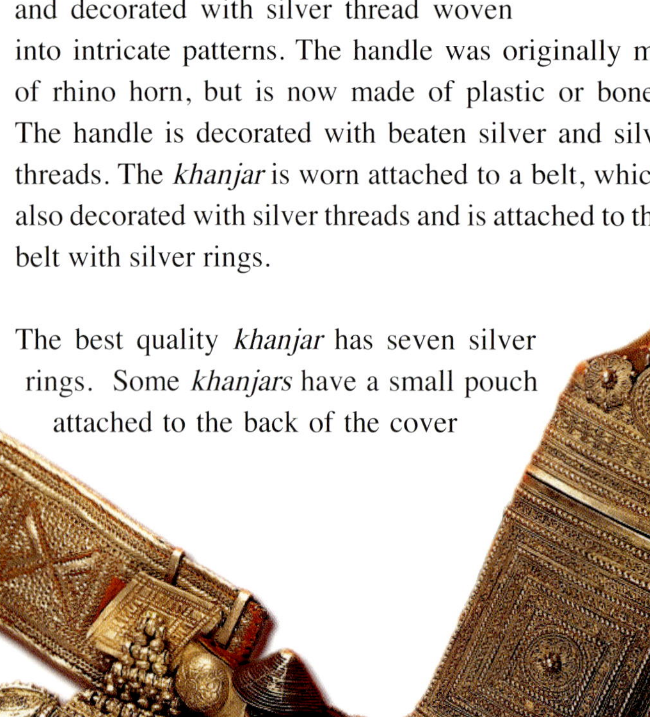

where a small knife is kept. This knife is for use with food rather than for protcction.

There is another design of *khanjar* known as the Al Saidi Khanjar that is worn by members of the Omani Royal family. This has a different shaped handle. In the Al Saidi Khanjar, the handle is smaller and is in a pointed cross shape entirely covered with silver.

A *khanjar* is never worn with the embroidered headdress know as the *kumah.* It is only worn with the *mussar,* a woven head cloth worn in a similar fashion to a turban. Some men wear the *khanjar* and belt and then cover the belt with a *shal made* of the same material as the *mussar.*

National Costumes

Omani national costumes differ from region to region especially for women, though there are also differences in men's clothing.

In Salalah, in the south of Oman, the women wear a long loose-fitting velvet dress over pantaloons. The dress is shorter at the front than it is at the back so the back forms a little train that brushes away her footsteps as she walks in the sand.

Salalah Style

In the northern part of the country in the Batinah region, the ladies wear a brightly coloured knee-length *dishdasha* over pantaloons. The pantaloons are called *sirwaal* and are usually embroidered at the ankles. The women cover their hair with a scarf, called a *lahaf,* which may be black, or multi-coloured, and then over the complete outfit they wear a black cloak called an *abaya.* The *abaya,* however, is imported and not a traditional robe, having been introduced within the last thirty years or so. The *abaya* has been so engrained into today's modern dress that it is now a fashion statement and many elaborate designs are sold to young women.

Balushi Style

In the Dhahirah region of Ibri and Buraimi, ladies wear a full-length *dishdasha* over their *sirwaal* and cover their hair with a black *lahaf.* In Sur, in the Sharqiya region, ladies wear a loosely woven garment called a *qaba'a* over their *sirwaal* and knee-length *dishdasha.* The *qaba'a,* usually black or red, is used to cover the head instead of an *abaya.* In many regions, women choose to wear a veil and this too varies in design according to the region. Some are made of fine netting and cover the whole face, as in the Sur region where the veil is called

Batinah Region

ghashawah. The mask that is worn by some Bedouin ladies is called a *burka* and may be made in different styles. Purple, bronze and gold are the favorite colours for the *burka* and all are made using burnished indigo to dye the fabric.

Suri Style

In the capital area around Muscat, it is possible to see local women wearing two kinds of traditional dress; the Muscati dress and the Lawati dress. The Muscati dress is a short *dishdasha* worn over matching *sirwaal* trousers, but the *lahaf* is of contrasting colours and usually edged with elaborate designs. The Lawati dress is an ankle-length *dishdasha* with bands of gold and silver embroidery at the hemline, and is worn over *sirwaal* trousers that have an embroidered cuff at the ankle. The *lahaf* is edged with gold or silver tassels.

Whatever the region, the costumes of Omani women are a striking contrast to the sandy coloured plains and mountains.

Dishdasha with Kumah

Omani men wear a *dishdasha*, a simple long white cotton robe with long sleeves. The sleeves are loose at the cuff unlike the *dishdasha* worn in some of the other Gulf States. The neck is a simple round neck without a collar and there is a button and a tassel, sometimes called a *kashcusha* or a *fareekha,* which hangs at the right side of the neck.

The *kashcusha* is where Omani men spray their perfume and whenever they enter an area that does not have a very pleasant smell; they hold the tassel up to their noses and inhale the pleasant smell of the perfume. Under their *dishdasha*, men wear a simple piece of cloth called a *wizar.* This is wrapped around the body from the waist to the ankles.

Dishdasha with mussar and Khanjar

There are two main headdresses worn by Omani men, one is the kumah, an embroidered cap that is handmade and often embroidered by the women

Sharqiyqh Region

in the family, and the other is the *mussar*, which is a brightly coloured and patterned shawl that is worn like a turban. Members of the Royal family wear a special turban for ceremonial occasions made of brightly coloured cloth woven in the Sharqiya region.

Omani men wear sandals called *na'al* instead of socks and shoes, as these are much cooler for the feet.

For ceremonial occasions, men wear a curved silver dagger called a *khanjar* which is held in place by a belt woven with silver threads and this is sometimes covered with a

woollen stole called a *shal.* The *shal* is always the same colour as the *mussar.* The *khanjar* is never worn with a *kumah.*

In Sur the *dishdasha* is slightly different to the other regions. There the men's *dishdasha* is gathered down the front and across the shoulder seam at the front and back and at the sleeve. In Ibri and Buraimi there are slight differences too, the *kashcusha* is either often very long or there is no *kashcusha* at all, and the *mussar* is either plain white, or red and white checks.

Currency & Postage stamps

Before the introduction of coins, bartering, or offering goods and services in exchange for other goods, was the way that people bought and sold things in Oman, and throughout much of the world.

The first coins used in Oman were issued from the mint in 700 AD.
In 1970, at the time when His Majesty came to the throne, the currency, coins and paper notes were known as the Sa'idi Rial. His Majesty Sultan Qaboos introduced the currency that we use today, the Omani Rial, in 1971.

History tells us that in the past, the Maria Theresa dollar named after the Austrian Empress Maria Theresa, and Indian rupees were legal currency in Oman.

Present Day Currency

Maria Theresa dollar

The silver Maria Theresa dollar can still be found today in silver and antique shops in the souqs of Oman. In some cases, this has been made into jewellery.

The first post office opened in Muscat in 1856. Until 1947, Indian postage stamps were used. After 1947, when India gained its independence from Britain, British postage stamps were used in Oman. The first Omani postage stamps were issued in 1966.

Oman issues some of the most beautiful commemorative postage stamps in the world and they are much sought after by collectors all over the world.

Many of the themes used on the stamps illustrate Oman's culture, history and wildlife. If you don't already collect stamps, this is a wonderful opportunity to begin a hobby that could attract interest and friends from all over the world.

Omani Stamps

Dhows

Oman and her people have a strong maritime heritage both as sailors and ship builders. Over 500 years ago in 1498 one of Oman's best known sailors Ahmed bin Majid sailed with the Portuguese explorer, Vasco da Gama to the Orient. Omani's believe that the fabled explorer Sindbad was born in Sohar, a town 230 kilometers north of Muscat. Sindbad's adventures are recorded in the book of One Thousand and One Arabian Nights.

To the south of Muscat 330 kilometers away is the town of Sur which has been the hub of ship building in Oman for hundreds of years. Sur was once a trading centre for slaves and cloves from East Africa, but it is for its success as a ship building centre that has earned Sur its place in Omani and world history books.

The ship yards and their skilled craftsmen together with the famous Dhows they have built have made Sur famous. Traditional Dhows were made from Teak imported from India and were originally sewn together with ropes made from coconut fibers. No nails at all were used. Tim Severin a British explorer decided to re-create one of the fabled voyages of Sindbad and built a copy of an original dhow using traditional methods. Suitable trees were selected in India and the wood brought to Oman – a staggering 140 metric tons. 600 kilometers of handmade rope were used to sew the planks of wood together and the holes drilled used ancient tools were sealed with lime and vegetable oil to protect the wood from salt water. The journey from Oman to China, 10,000 kilometers in all, took 1 1/2 years. Tim Severin began his journey to Canton in China in 1980 as part of Oman's 10th National Day celebrations.

The dhow was called the *Sohar,* and now stands on the roundabout at the entrance to the Al Bustan Palace Hotel.

Almost thirty years later Oman once again embarked on a pioneering maritime project. In 2010 a replica of a 9th century sewn plank ship, built at Qantab near Muscat, set sail from Muscat to Singapore. The *"Jewel of Muscat"* was a gift from the Omani people to the people of Singapore and was a reconstruction of the Belitung shipwreck discovered in 1998

Work began on the *Jewel,* at the beginning of 2008 when a model of the ship was built. In June of that year special trees were selected in Ghana to be used for the keel and the planks. In October 2008 the wood arrived in Muscat at the specially built construction site at Qantab. In October 2009 *Jewel,* was ready to launch and in February 2010 she set sail for Singapore. On the first part of her journey *Jewel* was in dry dock in Cochin in India having spent 28 days at sea covering a distance 2092 kilometers. From India, Jewel sailed to Sri Lanka and then on to Malaysia before finally docking in Singapore, having retraced part of the historic maritime trading routes used by sailors from Arabia to the Far East. *Jewel* finally reached Singapore on the 3rd July 2010.

Once again traditional construction methods were used. No nails at all were used; it took 120 kilometers of handmade coir rope made from coconut fibers and 70,000 stitches to sew the boat together. The wooden planks were covered in goat fat mixed with lime to protect the wood from the salt water. In all 15 metric tons of African hardwood, 5 metric tons of teak, 1 ton of poona wood and 1 ton of Omani sidr wood were needed to made *the Jewel.* The sails were made of palm leaf and cover an area of 160 square meters.

After almost 5 months at sea His Majesty's gift was handed over to the people of Singapore. At the Asian Civilization Museum she was part of an exhibition to celebrate the 40th Renaissance day on 23rd July 2010. *Jewel* is now housed permanently in a maritime museum in Singapore.

Jewel of Muscat

The Falaj

The Falaj system is a unique way of transporting water. It is a system of small, man-made channels used to carry water from an upland reservoir to villages and farms below.

Local legend claims that Solomon, the son of David, visited Oman on a flying carpet and made the jinns or evil spirits construct 10,000 water channels in just 10 days. In a falaj system the distribution of water flowing through the channels is strictly controlled as many people share the water. Priorities are set for the use of water. The first priority is given to drinking water taken from the point nearest to the source. Next is the bathing area. The men's bathing area is higher up the channel than the women's bathing area. Water used in the ceremonial washing of the dead is next and finally water for watering plants and crops.

The feeder channels that direct the flow of water to fields are opened and closed to allow water to flow only at the time agreed by the community. A sundial in the village is used to determine when and how long this time will be. The aflaj need to be cleaned and maintained regularly so that there is no pollution, and the whole village shares this task.

Omani Flag & National Anthem

The Omani Flag is red, white and green, and was adopted as the National flag in December 1970. The national emblem is shown on the flag on the red nearest to the flagpole. This shows crossed swords and a khanjar, the traditional weapons of the Omani people.

The colours used in the flag are symbolic.

The old Omani flag was all red. The red in the new flag demonstrates continuity and respect for past battles that were fought and the blood spilled trying to evict foreign invaders from Oman.

The green represents the fertility of the land and the white is for peace and the conviction of the Omani people to live in peace and prosperity.

The National Anthem, in translation

"Oh Allah, protect for us His Majesty the Sultan"

Oh Allah, protect for us His Majesty the Sultan,
And the people in our land;
With honour and peace;
May he live long and be supported,
May his leadership be glorious,
For him we shall lay down our lives;
Oh Oman - since the time of the Prophet,
We are a dedicated people amongst the noble Arabs,
Rejoice - Qaboos has come,
With the blessings of Heaven;
Take courage and protect him with your prayers.

Forts

There are over five hundred forts, watchtowers and castles in Oman, and many of these have been rebuilt and restored by the Government. They were built for protection on hills and mountains overlooking villages and seaports.

Al Hazm Fort

The Portuguese built some of these forts in the early 16th century. The most famous forts in Muscat are Fort Mirani, which was completed almost 500 years ago in 1587, and its twin, Fort Jelali. Mirani and Jelali were built high on the rocks in Muscat and guard His Majesty's Palace in Muscat, *Al Alam Palace* and the city of Muscat. Fort Jelali was used as a prison until the early 1970's, but it is now a museum.

Muttrah Fort is situated on the Corniche, just a short way from the city of Muscat and was restored at the end of the 1970's.

Jabreen Fort

Bait Al Falaj Fort in Ruwi, built in 1806, is now the home of the Armed Forces Museum. The fort at Nizwa, which was once the capital city of Oman, was built in the mid-17th century. It has a circular tower that provides 360 degree visibility of the town below. This is the biggest fort in the Arabian Peninsula. The fort at Bahla, called Hisn Tamah, was named after the chief who built it and has a wall approximately 11 kms long, which was patrolled night and day by sentries. UNESCO has Bahla Fort on their list of World Heritage Sites.

Jabrin Fort, once the palace of Imam Bil'Arab bin Sultan, was built in the mid-17th century. This fort has wonderful Islamic and floral patterns painted on its wooden ceilings and beams. There are false floors and secret passages and it even has its own quran school in one of the upper rooms and a special room for the Imam's favourite horse!

Forts have played a very important role in the history of Oman and to acknowledge this, they appear on some bank notes and on postage stamps.

Bahla Fort

Nakhal Fort

Frankincense and Myrrh

Frankincense, the gift of kings, more precious than gold, has humble beginnings as the sap of a tree in the Dhofar region of Southern Oman. The *Boswellia* tree is not even a very pretty tree but it grows abundantly in Dhofar region, and gave rise to one of the most important trading activities of ancient times in the region.

To collect the frankincense the bark is shaved off the tree trunk using a special knife and as the bark is removed sap called *Luban*, a resin like substance oozes from the tree trunk. It is almost as if the tree was bleeding from the cuts inflicted in the bark. The *Luban* hardens into crystals and it is the crystals that are collected and sold as frankincense.

Frankincense continues to be used today and is the base of many of the world's most expensive perfumes. Oman's most famous and most expensive perfume *Amouage*, uses frankincense as one of the main ingredients. Frankincense is used in Arabia to welcome guests into a home, at weddings and at official functions as well as during religious festivals. The frankincense crystals when burned, gives off a pleasant, fragrant, sometimes heady smell. Ancient tribes and communities all over the region believed the fragrant white smoke from burning incense soothed angry gods.

The Emperor Nero burned an entire year's production of incense from Arabia at the funeral of his wife Poppaea. Frankincense was also used for embalming dead bodies, but because of the high price of frankincense this would only have been used for the rich and famous. For example frankincense was discovered in the tomb King Tutankhamen, but this was to be expected given his status as king. The ancient Greeks used frankincense to treat hemorrhoids and it continues to be used today in some medicines. In today's modern world frankincense is used in the west as aromatherapy oil where it is said to have many properties. It is still of course

used for meditation and spiritual work, but the essential oil can be used as an anti inflammatory, anti -depressant and antiseptic. It is often used in medicines for the respiratory system or asthma and has a calming effect so provides inner peace.

The frankincense grown in and around Salalah is some of the best quality and therefore the most expensive in the world. Though frankincense grows in other areas of the world such as India and Somalia, there are known to be 25 different types of *Boswellia* tree, but it is the *Boswellia Sacra* that produces the best quality frankincense and this is found only in Oman. The frankincense trees of Wadi Dawkah and the remains of the caravan oasis of Shisr/Wubar and the ports of Khor Rori and Al-Baleed illustrate the trade in Frankincense that flourished in the region for many centuries.

The lost city of Ubar, recently rediscovered by archaeologists near Salalah was thought to be the central warehouse for frankincense on the famous *'frankincense trail.'* In ancient times frankincense from Salalah was traded with the Romans and the Greeks and the legendary Queen of Sheba is said to have travelled to Salalah to buy her frankincense. Frankincense is mentioned in the Bible as one of the gifts the three kings took to the baby Jesus in Bethlehem. Why they took frankincense is not understood by many people. The reason is that frankincense was valued as high if not higher than gold or jewels. An Arab historian suggests that frankincense was taken as one of the gifts for Jesus because, *"the smoke of incense reaches heaven as does no other smoke..."*

The frankincense trail began in Dhofar in Salalah, where the frankincense was either sent by ship or overland on camel trains to the rest of the world. For over 2000 years frankincense has been the basis of the economy of Salalah. It was the rise in the sale of frankincense that caused the ancient port of Sumharam to be built in the second century. The King of the Hadramaut tribe (now in Yemen) held the monopoly at that time for the frankincense trade and it is Sumharam that is part of the UNESCO World Heritage site, recognized in 2000.

Sadly, there are at this time fake frankincense crystals being sold. In the mid 20th century another chemically engineered crystal was developed which smells just like frankincense. This has been introduced into the world market and is much cheaper than frankincense, but has affected the volume of sales of the real resin and fragrance.

Today there is still a frankinsence suq in Salalah and many families continue to make their living selling and cultivating the *Boswellia Sacra* tree and living off its fragrance. To demonstrate just how much frankincense is revered as part of the history and culture of the region there are vast incense burners decorating road sides, and roundabouts some acting as fountains and others with smoke curling up into the sky. Sometimes the decorative incenses burners are used as plant pots and are filled with petunias or other flowers. Salalah has a thriving industry making decorative incense burners though today there are many imported or electronic burners, but most people, tourists and residents alike, still prefer the burners from Salalah.

Though once said to be more precious than gold, frankincense now sells in the UK for instance at the following rate, 50 gms of the best quality frankincense - *Royal Hougari* is 14.00 pounds sterling. Today in Oman frankincense sticks are available. Hand made in Oman these are similar to *joss -sticks* and burn for almost 2 hours and are a fragrant and inexpensive way to enjoy frankincense.

Myrrh – Sometimes called the *balm of Gilead,* comes from the *Commiphora Myrrha* tree. It was also one of the gifts the wise men took to baby Jesus. It was also used to relief the pain of prisoners about to die and Jesus is recorded as being given a sponge soaked with wine and myrrh as he hung on the cross.

In ancient Rome, myrrh was priced five times higher than frankincense but today sells in the UK for very much less, 50 gms of myrrh can be bought for 9.00 pounds sterling.

Myrrh originated from and is still largely only available in the Arabian Peninsula, but there are also trees in

Somalia. Its trade routes reached Jerusalem and Egypt from modern Oman which was then known as the Dhofar Region and Yemen. The writings of classical scholars tell us much about the past history of the region. In the 5th century BC, Herodotus wrote, "*Arabia is the only country which produces myrrh, frankincense, cassia and cinnamon.*" *An earlier author records that, "all of Arabia exudes a most delicious fragrance, and even passing seamen can smell the strong fragrance that gives health and vigor."*

The ancient Romans burnt myrrh on their funeral pyres to mask the smell of the burning corpses. They used it as an antiseptic and also used Myrrh to fumigate wine jars before bottling thus adding a luxurious flavour to the wine. It is still used today to make *Fermet* a liqueur popular for flavoring coffee especially in Italy or may be used to sooth colic in babies. Today Myrrh is used as a medicine and a large percentage of Arab households use myrrh as a medicinal aid. It is commonly used in toothpaste, mouthwash and as a liniment for aches and bruises the world over.

Myrrh

Frankincense burner on the roundabout at Wadi Khabir

Frankincense burner, typical northern Oman design, seen on the Corniche at Muttrah.

Frankincense burners, typical Dhofari design, based on a cube shape and hand made.

A local tradesman displays his frankincense in Muttrah souq.

Mosques

Mosques in Oman are magnificent and one of the most beautiful and breathtaking is the Sultan Qaboos Grand Mosque inaugurated in May 2001. It is located in Bausher on the main Muscat to Seeb highway. The Grand Mosque complex is made up of a mosque, an Islamic library and an Institute for Islamic studies.

The Mosque was a gift from His Majesty Sultan Qaboos to the people of Oman. It took six years to build and the total complex covers an area of 416,000 square metres. The actual mosque covers an area of 40,000 square metres and has 16,000 square metres of hand-carved stonework on the walls. The dome is 50 metres tall. The marble used in the construction was imported from Italy and Iran. There are 35 crystal chandeliers and the central chandelier weighs 8,500 kgs and is 14 metres long.

The minarets, one tall and four smaller ones represent the Five Pillars of Islam. The prayer mat, a single woven carpet, weighs 21,000 kgs, and covers an area of 263 square metres. It is made up of 1,700,000,000 knots and took 4 years to produce. It was woven in Iran where 600 female workers wove the threads and tied the knots that make up

Sultan Qaboos Grand Mosque, Ghalla

the carpet. The Mosque allows 20,000 people to worship at one time in the facilities provided.

Wealthy families and leading businessmen have built many of the mosques in Oman.

Oman was one of the earliest countries to accept Islam and there are two mosques in Nizwa thought to belong to that period dating back to the second year of the Al Hijra calendar about 624 AD.

Most Omanis are Ibadi Muslims, though there are some Sunnis and a small number of Shia.

The Biblical Old Testament Prophet, Job or Ayyoub in Arabic, is buried in a tomb to the north of Salalah. A new mosque has been built beside the original mosque tomb and this is one of the major tourist attractions of the Salalah region as well as a place of pilgrimage for Muslims.

Tomb of the Prophet Job, Salalah

Grand Rasoul Mosque

Silver & Gold

Silver has been used in Oman for 4000 years. It was the principle symbol of wealth in the past, but has been overtaken by the need for gold.

Silver was believed to have magical powers and to help ward off the evil eye. Mercury was also believed to have magical powers and was used by the Bedouin in the interior. It was rubbed onto the gums of babies to protect them from evil.

Nizwa, once the capital of Oman, is still famous for the work of its silversmiths. Traditional jewellery was always made from silver, but in recent times gold jewellery has become more popular. Omani women wear all their jewellery at once which almost makes a lady a walking bank account as a man attaches his wealth to the wrists, neck and ankles of his wife. The whole family owns some of the very expensive pieces, such as a headdress or hand jewellery.

Anklets are given to a girl at puberty and are worn until she marries. Anklets and sometimes bracelets are often filled with sand, seeds or small stones so that they make

a jangling sound when the wearer moves. These are then used to form the basic rhythm when dancing.

Rings are worn on both the hands and feet. Toe rings are quite simple pieces of jewellery, but finger rings are very ornate and distinct, with a special ring and shape for each of the five fingers. A set of ten finger rings is often given as a wedding gift.

Necklaces sometimes include a Quran holder, in which a verse from the Quran is placed to protect the wearer from evil.

Earrings are often very large, with as many as four pairs worn at one time. When five or more pairs of earrings are worn together, a special headband supports the weight of the earrings.

Souqs

In Oman, as in many other countries, the *souq* or market place is much more than a place of business. It is a social gathering place, a place to see and be seen.

The *souq* may sell mouth-watering fruits and vegetables, local handicrafts, fresh fish, goats and livestock, souvenirs or oriental spices.

A treasure trove of object d'art in Muttrah souq

The *souq* in Muttrah, with its main entrance off the Corniche, is a *must visit* place for anyone who lives in or visits Oman. It has been modernized, but it is still a magical place.

It has lots of narrow alleyways where some traders still sit on the floor at the entrance to their shops with their goods piled up behind them from floor to ceiling in a narrow shop.

Everyone receives a warm welcome in Muttrah souq, even the cat, seen here relaxing amongst the sounds and smells of the souq

It is like stepping back in time as you wander through the alleyways. You will find the largest cooking pots that you have ever seen, traditional medicines, gold and silver, souvenirs, T-shirts, clothes, toys and stationery, fabrics, traditional handicrafts, Bedouin jewellery and artifacts.

Every town has its own traditional *souq.* In Nizwa, the *souq* is situated beside Nizwa Fort. Here there is still an opportunity to see traditional craftsmen making khanjars and jewellery in silver. The best traditional silversmiths come from the Nizwa region, so the workmanship is of the best quality. Pottery can be bought from nearby Bahla.

Tourists from visiting cruise ships flock to the local souqs

Camels

Camel breeding and rearing is a traditional activity practiced all over Oman, dating back to references in the Holy Quran. The camels found in Oman are *Dromedaries* – with one hump which is indigenous to the Middle East, North Africa and India. *Bactrian's* have two humps and are found mainly in central Asia.

Omani camels are of medium size and known for their strength and speed. The colour of the camels varies from region to region. In the south, in Salalah most of the camels are black, the lighter- sandy coloured – the more common colour for camels are found elsewhere. Camels are used in Oman for riding or racing and also for meat and milk. Camel-breeding has become more profitable in recent years and therefore more popular; the price of a racing camel can reach over Omani Rials 75,000. Approx US $200,000-

His Majesty Sultan Qaboos is keen to preserve all aspects of traditional heritage and culture and so a Directorate General of Camel Affairs was established in the Diwan of Royal Court in 1989. This is located in the wilayat of Barka at Fulaij, and is equipped with the most modern race tracks and camel pens.

Omani dromedaries

Many people refer to camels as the ships of the desert not because they have been used for thousands of years to transport people and goods across vast areas of desert, but because they walk like a giraffe and move both legs on the same side of their body at the same time so they roll from side to side as they walk, just like a ship rolls.

To the Bedouin who still live a nomadic lifestyle, camels are more than that. The Bedouin call the camel - *Ata Allah, or God's gift.*

This is why. The camels provide transport, the hair of the camel is used to weave clothing, blankets and mats, and camel milk is very nutritious and is used for drinking and in the preparation of other foods. The hide may be used to make tents or mats or gourds for carrying water and the meat can be eaten. Even camel dung can be used to burn on a fire as a source of heat in the cooler desert nights, and sometimes the bones of dead camels are used to make jewellery and replaces ivory.

Camels have a reputation of being moody and are known to spit at people they do not like, but they are also quite smart. To stay as cool as possible in the desert, when resting they turn away from the sun and lie with either their heads or tails facing the sun so that the sun reaches only the smallest part of their bodies.

Today when transporting camels from one area to another or to a race, camels are moved by truck and it is quite common to see a camel tied down in the back on an

open topped pick up. I say common, but to me it is also comical to see this. On such occasions the camel's head and ears are covered so that they do not feel the cold and often a crocheted bag, a mouth guard, covers the mouth.

A camel in the desert seems to move very slowly and sedately; and why not in temperatures of 40 – 50 degrees celsius? However, those camels bred for racing can reach very fast speeds. A camel can run at speeds of up to 64 kms an hour, but this is only for short distances. At 40 kms. an hour they can run for 1 hour and by reducing the speed to 19 kms an hour they can run for 18 hours. When running a camel actually appears to have all 4 hooves off the ground at the same time as it flies through the air pushing towards the finish line. It is interesting to note that most of the racing camels are female. Racing camels bred and trained in Oman are much in demand by Sheiks from the UAE and can earn their owners lots of money. It is however expensive to keep a racing camel as their normal diet of thorny scrub and leaves is not good enough for a high performance camel. Well cared for racing camels are often fed the finest honey and dates, fresh cow's milk, wheat and fresh alfalfa grass. Mouth-guards ensure that the animals do not graze on desert vegetation, in case they lose their stamina and consequently their racing prowess.

The name *Dromedary* is usually used to refer to racing camels. They can travel for 130 kms a day carrying a rider, not of course in a race, but walking long distances such as those required by the Camel Corp on their military patrols.

The '*beast of burden,'* camel used for transporting goods is a much sturdier beast than a racing camel and can carry as much as 200 kgs for about 60 kms a day.

The camel is not a very pretty beast, but to me a fascinating creature. Here are a few facts - The Arabian camel can weigh between 500 – 700 kgs and stands approx 2 meters high at the shoulder. The legs are long and nobly kneed with hooves that have 2 big toes with a calloused pad beneath. The feet can be as big as plates and this helps them to walk without sinking into the sand. There is a cleft in the upper lip and the eyes have long thick lashes to protect them from the sun and the sand. They also have a third eyelid that closes from the side to help to protect the eyes from blowing sand, or to wash out and sand that does get in the eye. However they are able to see through this third eyelid so sometimes a camel will closes its eyes in a sand storm but still be able to see where it is going. A camel can close its nostrils to keep out sand in a storm and the lips are thickened to protect them from the course desert plants that they feed on. A camel has really small hairy ears and this too is protection against the sand in a storm.

A camel can and will drink any sort of water, from clean, to brackish to salty if need be, and will eat anything. The usual diet is the vegetation that can be found in the desert but if they are hungry a camel will eat fish, meat, skin and bones. A popular misconception about camels is where they store their water. Most people believe that this is stored in the hump but this is not so. Camels store water in their hooves. The hump is used to store fatty tissue which can be used as a source of energy later.

Fish & Marine Life

Most of us probably don't think about fish, unless it is on the menu at a restaurant. We might like to eat fish or we might like to go fishing for sport or relaxation, but for Oman, fish is more than just sport and food.

The fish and marine life in the seas around Oman's coastline provide jobs for fishermen, food for local residents, food to export and are a tourist attraction as Oman's dive sites become more and more popular. Fish also provide income for the fishermen and the national economy.

There are over 150 species of fish in the seas around Oman. There are tiny sardines and enormous whales and almost everything in between.

There are also pods (groups) of whales and dolphins. Sometimes all you have to do is stand on the beach to see pods of both whales and dolphins swimming off the coast. Local fishermen think of the dolphins as friends and a sign of good luck as

Fusilier fish

the fishermen know that they are likely to find tuna fish wherever they see pods of dolphins.

Whales, dolphins and turtles are a major tourist attraction in Oman. Though it is possible to stand of the seashore and observe pods of dolphins and whales, especially in Salalah many companies operate short whale and dolphin watching tours which are extremely popular. The dolphins are not at all afraid of the camera clicking tourists and many swim alongside and underneath the boats. Dolphins are sleek and graceful and highly intelligent and have featured in numerous myths and legends the world over.

Bat fish

The humpback whale is most interesting in Oman as it feeds and breeds in Oman's waters. Everywhere else it is migratory, moving from breeding grounds in warm waters to feeding grounds in colder polar waters. The monsoon season in the summer months in the south of Oman provides conditions that are perfect for feeding and breeding. The sperm whale and blue whale are also to be seen off the coast of Oman.

Banner fish

Turtles

Oman has some of the most important sea turtle nesting beaches in the world, and in the case of the loggerhead turtle, probably the most important. In 1977 the first survey of turtles in Oman was carried out by many international institutions including WWF. The survey and subsequent tagging of species of turtles showed that the turtles around 23,000 which were tagged, cover vast distances between nesting periods but almost always return to the beach where their hatched to nest.

There are 5 species of sea turtles that occur in Oman, four of which nest here: Green (*Chelonia mydas*) -which is endangered; Loggerhead (*Caretta caretta*); Olive Ridley (*Lepidochelys olivacea)* - the smallest; Hawksbill (*Eretmochelys imbricata)*; Leatherback (*Dermochelys coriacea)*- the largest and a visitor only in offshore waters.

Sea turtles nest along the length of the Omani coast from Musandam in the north to Dhofar in the south, but Ras Al Hadd (the most easterly point of Oman) south of the ancient sea port of Sur, is famous for its green turtles. Masirah Island attracts the loggerhead turtle in vast number, and on the Daymaniyat Islands the hawksbill turtles set the record.

Conservation of turtles is high on the list of priorities in Oman:

All beaches in the Ras Al Hadd area are closed to campers, with the exception of Ras Al Junayz where a campsite has been opened, out of sight of the sea, in order not to disturb the turtles. A permit (for a small fee) is required to visit this site, and guides take campers down to the nesting grounds to watch the turtles come ashore and lay their eggs at night. The main nesting period, when a female turtle can lay up to one hundred eggs, is between June and September. A female turtle born in the sands of Ras Al Hadd or on the beaches of Masirah Island will return to that same beach thirty or thirty-five years later, and each year after that, to lay her eggs.

Once the hatchlings leave the nest to make their way to the sea, they are in extreme danger. The sight of a hatchling making its way to the sea means breakfast to a waiting seagull or crab. A fox may also be lying in wait for a free meal, and so of the hundred or so eggs laid by a female, perhaps only twenty actually make it to the sea. Once they are in the sea the hatchlings are still not safe, as some species of fish will use the opportunity to snatch a snack. Many turtles and hatchlings get caught up each year in fishing nets.

Wildlife

Oman is blessed with an abundance of wildlife. Many people think only of camels when they think of the wildlife of Arabian Gulf countries, but there is much more to interest nature lovers than just our Dromedaries.

Bird watchers and ornithologists come to Oman to observe the hundreds of species of birds who are either native to these shores or use Oman as a staging post as they migrate north or south. There are almost 500 species of birds recorded as being spotted in Oman.

White Arabian Oryx

Some of the more popular birds are the Indian Roller, the Hoopoe seen as it migrates in February, and Bustards, often seen in central Oman. The Imperial Eagle visits Oman between autumn and early spring. Several species of Vultures are seen regularly and are very common in northern Oman. Sooty Gulls are a common sight on Masirah Island as the birds migrate from March to October and Salalah is famous for its Pink Flamingos. These are of course just a few of

Flamingo

Hoopoe

Purple Sunbird

the birds in Oman.

When we think of the mammals of the region we may perhaps think of the White Arabian Oryx, the Arabian Leopard, the Tahr and the Caracal Lynx, but there are many more species. There are Porcupines, Hedgehogs, Honey Badgers, White Tailed Mongoose, Hares, Sand Cats, Nubian Ibox, Sand Gazelles, Foxes, Arabian Wolves, Spotted Genet and wild cats. Many of these species live in the mountains of the Dhofar region.

The white Oryx, once roamed freely in Arabia, but was almost hunted to the point of extinction. Some of the last remaining Oryx were sent to San Diego Zoo in America where they were successfully bred in captivity and were returned to Oman in 1980 to start new herds.

A special sanctuary was set up for the Oryx in Jiddat Al Harasis in central Oman. The Oryx is a very beautiful animal with a white coat, black legs and long pointed horns.

The Tahr or mountain goat is found only in Northern Oman and in some parts of the United Arab Emirates. It has very distinctive horns and a beard, but is easily distinguishable from its cousin the goat. Hunting the Tahr is banned in Oman and rangers

patrol mountainous regions to make sure that traps are destroyed and that the Tahr is protected. The last remaining Arabian leopards can be found in the extreme north of Oman in Musandam and in the mountains of the southern region of Dhofar.
Great efforts are being made to save this big cat from extinction. The Red Fox is common in coastal areas and is abundant in Ras Al Hadd, but these are also seen near residential areas and even in cities. The Arabian Wolf is most common in the mountains of Dhofar and in northern Oman. Small, very shy Ethiopian H edgehogs inhabit the northern mountains and can sometimes be seen in the Batinah region. The Honey Badger, the Striped Hyena, Arabian Leopard and the White Tailed Mongoose

are native to the Dhofar Mountains. The sands of the Jiddat Al Harasis famous for the Arabian White Oryx is also home to the Hyrax, the Sand Cat, the Sand Gazelle, the Caracal Lynx and the Arabian Gazelle.

Oman is home to many species of butterflies, and some of them with some exotic names such as, the Desert Orange Tip, the Salmon Arab, Pomegranate Butterfly, Asian Grass Blue, Blue Pansy, Grass Jewel, Fig Blue, Scarlet Tip and Pea Blue. A large number of the butterflies in Oman inhabit the mountains of Jebal Akhdar where the weather is cooler and the fruits and flowers that grow there provide the habitats that the butterfly and their larvae feed on. Some of the more common butterflies can be found in Muscat, Musandam and in the Dhofar region.

Blue spotted Arab

Tiger butterfly

A sandy, shaded garden or even our own homes can provide nesting places for rodents, snakes, scorpions and gekkos. Most of these are harmless and, in fact, provide free cleaning services by eating the mosquitoes, but some of us are frightened by them and would prefer not to have to deal with them as guests in our homes and gardens. Scorpions can live without food for more than a year and sense their prey through tiny movements in the ground.

Blue-Pansy

Lime butterfly

Horses and Equestrian sports

Omani's love their horses, horse racing and equestrian events many of which are attended by members of the Royal family, Government Ministers and officials.

Horse racing attracts local as well as expatriate audiences as there is always more than just the *race*, which is common in Europe. One obvious distinction is the fact that there is no gambling. Owners, trainers, riders and spectators gather at these events for the love of the sport not the cash rewards from placing a bet. There are however prizes awarded to owners and jockeys, sometimes prizes as grand as a new car.

Besides the races, riders participate in polo matches, tent-pegging competitions, trotting races, and show-jumping, dressage and carriage processions. Women participate in some of these events and the Royal Oman Cavalry has female horse riders many of whom join the cavalry from a very young age.

History tells us that Oman has a long association with horses. In the 14th century Ibn Battuta the famous Moroccan explorer mentions in his writings that thoroughbred horses were exported from Dhofar in the south of Oman. Marco Polo, writing

earlier, in the 13th century, also refers to the export of fine Arabian horses from Qalhat and Dhofar.

Oman currently has about 2,000 horses, of which approximately 350 are pure-bred Arab horses, 150 are thoroughbreds and 1,500 are pure-bred Omani horses. The Omanis' love of horses can be seen in the way they deck them out: the neck ornaments, the silver bridle, the sweat blanket placed on the back and the under-cloth to prevent chafing, the silver collar-piece, and finally the reins.

His Majesty the Sultan pays special attention to all aspects of horse-breeding, preserving bloodlines, and equestrian sports of all kinds. A Directorate-General of the Royal Stables has been established under the Diwan of Royal Court which

supervises the breeding and rearing of horses using scientific methods in conformity with international standards.

In addition, the Royal Horse Racing Club was established to oversee the planning and development of equestrian activities, as well as organising the Royal Oman Horse Show which is held every 5 years. The Racing Club also distributes horses every year to citizens who are prepared to care for them and organises the annual Royal Horse Race meeting which takes place under Royal patronage.

The Oman Equestrian Federation arranges other race meetings and equestrian events, with the aim of preserving this valuable heritage. The Royal Stables possess numerous breeds of horses known for their excellence in racing, dressage, show jumping and polo, in addition to a troupe of cavalry horses.

Caves in Oman

Al Hoota Cave and the Majlis Al Jinn

One of the joys of Al Hoota cave is that you do not need to be an intrepid explorer bouncing over dunes and rocks in a 4 wheel drive to enjoy the beauty of the cave. A regular saloon car and a drive of approx 2 hours from Muscat is all you need.

Officially opened to the public on the 36th National Day (2006) Al Hoota Cave, situated at the foot of Jebal Shams, is the first tourist cave in the Gulf region. You do not have to be interested in caving as such; you just need to be able to appreciate the wonders of nature.

This magnificent cave has been sculptured by the action of water on rock and provides a wonderful natural display of stalagmites and stalactites. On arrival at the site just outside Al Hamra, the intense heat, even in winter, is probably the first thing you notice. Once you have acclimatized take time to look around at the countryside before entering the reception area. Inside you will find a very well stocked gift shop, a coffee shop and restaurant, and a seating area. A small gauge electric train takes passengers from the reception area to the mouth of the cave, or in the event that the train is not working it is only a short walk (about 500mts) along the track and through the tunnel to the mouth of the cave. Incidentally this is the first train in Oman!

Al Hoota cave

Inside the cave, photography is not permitted but displays are well illuminated and the guides are very well informed and helpful. Well constructed walkways lead you through the cave and there are rest points at various places en route. The entire cave is not available to tourists, only the first 500 mts of the total 4.5 kms. can be accessed at this time. The walk around the cave takes approximately 40 minutes, but this trip is not for the faint hearted or those who need help walking as there are numerous steps to climb - 230 in total to reach the highest point. Because it is a cave it is very humid and this in itself makes the climb difficult at times. An underground lake inside the cave is home to blind, transparent fish that live on the organic nourishment carried by the rain water that drips into the cave. The main lake in the cave is around 800 mts long and about 10 mts in width, with a maximum depth of 15 mts.

Majlis Al Jinn.

The largest cave in Oman and the second largest in the world is the Majlis Al Jinn. At least this was the status of the cave when it was initially surveyed in 1985 but more recent records now place the cave as the 18th largest in the world with larger chambers having been discovered in more recent times.

Majlis Al Jinn

Omani legend informs us that the cave, situated on the Selma plateau on the north eastern coast of Oman in the Hajar Mountains was named, after Selma, a shepherdess who left her goats while she went to fetch water. When she returned she found a leopard eating her goats. She fought the leopard with an axe, but both she and the leopard were killed. Heaven sent down 7 stars to the spot where she was found and these became the 7 caves that now attract tourists from all over the world. The village and the plateau are now named after Selma.

To enjoy the Majlis al Jinn you need to be serious about caving, and have all of the protective equipment possible. The chamber of the cave is vast and could accommodate 10 jumbo jets parked side by side on the floor and stacked 4 deep. Or the great pyramid of Giza the largest in Egypt would almost fit into the cave. The cave's floor is bigger than the base of the pyramid but just not quite as tall as the pyramid. The floor of the cave is 58,000sq mts and the Majlis al Jinn has a volume is 4,000,000 cu.mts which by every definition is huge!

Only a few people have ever entered the cave as the entrance is from 3 rather insignificant holes in the roof. Depending on which hole you use the drop into the cave is between 120 and 158 mts to the cave floor and this makes it the longest free fall drop in Oman. Abseiling is the only way in!

UNESCO World Heritage Sites in Oman

Oman currently has four positions on the UNESCO list of World Heritage Sites with two more being consider at the moment. The World Heritage List was established in November 1972 and is concerned with the protection of culture and national heritage, something that is very close to the heart of Oman's leader H.M. Sultan Qaboos. Any site accepted by the World Heritage committee can be considered to be of outstanding universal value. The accepted sites are Bahla Fort, The Land of Frankincense, the Falaj Irrigation Systems of Oman and the Archaeological Sites of Bat, Al-Khutm and Al-Ayn

Bahla Fort is one of four historic forts found in the plains of Jebal Akhdar. There are forts at Bahla, Nizwa, Iski and Rustaq. Bahla fort was built between the 13th and 14th centuries. The oasis of Bahla owes its prosperity to the Banu Nebhan, the dominant tribe in the area from the 12th to the end of the 15th century. The fort's mud walls and towers rise some 165 feet above its sandstone foundations. The fort was not restored or conserved before 1987, and had fallen into disrepair, due to the rainy season each year, when the sandstone and mud would be washed away.

Rustaq fort

In 1987 Bahla fort became a UNESCO World Heritage Site. It was included in the List of World Heritage Sites in danger from 1988. Restoration work on the fort began in the 1990s, and the fort remained closed to tourists till work was completed in 2004 when it was removed from the endangered sites list.

The town of Bahla, including the oasis, souq and palm groves, is surrounded by mud walls approximately 12 kms long. Bahla is also famous for its pottery and jinn(magic)

The Frankincense Trail was added to the UNESCO World Heritage list in 2000. The complete site covers an area of just under 850,000 hectares. This includes the frankincense trees in Wadi Dawkah, the remains of the caravan oasis at Ubar in the district of Shisr and the ancient port of Khor Rori and Al Baleed. The immense area covered by this site testifies to the importance of the frankincense trade for this

region, one of the most important luxury items of trade in the ancient world. The Museum of the Land of Frankincense was officially opened on Renaissance day (July 23rd) 2007. It comprises 2 halls, a history hall and a maritime hall. There is also a viewing platform from which it is possible to see the many birds of the region visiting Al Baleed or the neighbouring lagoons. There are small boats for trips on the lagoon, a nursery for frankincense seedlings and a walkway along the northern bank of the lagoon.

Khor Rori (Sumhuram) approximately 40kms east of Salalah was once the best known port in the region for the trade of frankincense with the ancient world. Excavations show that this was a well defended, very prosperous town. Within the ruins earthenware pots

Frankincense trees in Salalah

have been found, cosmetic items and storage jars some in the style of vessels used by the Romans in the ancient world. On the edge of the Empty Quarter or the Rub al Khali, lies the ancient city of Ubar in the district of Shisr. There you will find the remains of an administrative building within the citadel.

The frankincense trees at Wadi Dawkah are located approximately 40 kms north of the city of Salalah on the way to Thumrait. There are 1230 mature trees with an additional 5000 trees being cultivated. The total area covers 14 square kms and lies in a semi desert wadi or river bed.

Falaj irrigation systems of Oman (2006)

The property includes five aflaj irrigation systems and is representative of some 3,000 such systems still in use in Oman. The origins of this system of irrigation may date back to AD 500, but archaeological evidence suggests that irrigation systems existed in this extremely arid area as early as 2500 BC. Using gravity, water is channeled from underground sources or springs to support agriculture and domestic use.

The fair and effective management and sharing of water in villages and towns is still underpinned by mutual dependence and communal values and guided by astronomical observations. Numerous watchtowers built to defend the water systems form part of the site reflecting the historic dependence of communities on the aflaj system. Threatened by falling levels of the underground water table, the aflaj represent an exceptionally well-preserved form of land use. Ancient engineering technologies demonstrate long standing, sustainable use of water resources for the cultivation of palms and other produce in extremely arid desert lands. Such systems reflect the former total dependence of communities on this irrigation and a time-honoured, fair and effective management and sharing of water resources.

Archaeological Sites of Bat, Al-Khutm and Al-Ayn Al Dhahirah region (1998)

The protohistoric site of Bat lies near a palm grove in the interior of the Sultanate of Oman. Together with the neighbouring sites, it forms the most complete collection of settlements and necropolises from the 3rd millennium B.C. in the world.

Two sites which are currently of the tentative list as World Heritage sites are, the forts at Rustaq and Al Hazm and the ancient city of Galhat. Both were listed as of 1988.

Bee-hive tombs at Bat

Rocks and Minerals

Oman must be paradise on earth for geologists. The landscape is spectacular and varied with mountains and deserts, beaches, rivers and waterfalls, bare rocks and lush green pastures. Some mountains rise 3,000 mts above sea level and in areas the sea bed is as low as 400 mts below sea level. It is believed that the countries rock formations span 825 million years. These include several periods when

the country was covered with ice; hard to believe in the harsh desert conditions that endure in some parts of Oman today. Underwater volcanoes formed the mountains; the Al Hajar range and the spectacular fjords of the Musandam Peninsular are evidence of this volcanic action.

Though most of Oman is now free of volcanic action the northern region of Musandam does occasionally feel tremors. Wind and water create beautiful features in the rocks and splendid examples can be found in sand dunes and in the rocks at Bandar Al Jissa where erosion by water has created undercut ledges that leave overhanging cliffs and arches. At Al Duqm nature has created some magnificent rock structures that artists would find difficult to recreate. The northern mountains are bare, but mountains in and around Salalah blossom and are covered with lush vegetation during and after the monsoon season each year. This is known locally as the Khareef Season and is a time of celebration and festivities. It is also a time when visitors from all of the Gulf States and Europe flock to the south of Oman in search of cooler weather.

The colours in the rocks in and around Muscat are breathtaking. A drive from Muscat over the mountains to Qantab, Al Jissa or the Oman Dive Centre reveals a splendid array of rock formations and colours, where shades of purple, green, red and grey blend together to create a brilliant canvas which an artist would feel privileged to use.

Oman's mountains are made up of volcanic, limestone and sedimentary rocks and store such minerals as gold, silver, marble, copper, iron, lead, chromium, gypsum, dolomite and limestone. Beneath the sands and the sea are countless fields of oil, often referred to as black gold, and natural gas. Much of Oman's wealth comes from its oil fields and natural gas.

Oman began exporting oil in 1967 and produces 813,000 barrels of oil a day. Oil production is measured in barrels, with approx. 160 lts in one barrel. As much as 90% of Oman's oil is exported, mainly to the Far East.

In prehistory Oman and Africa were joined and at some stage Oman was flooded by the sea. The warm waters of this region have abundant marine life and many fossils can be found in the rocks and on the shore as evidence of the flooding which took place. These decayed plants, bacteria and algae have all played their part in the production of oil. As these microscopic plants and organisms die they slowly sink to the bottom forming thick layers of organic material which are then covered in layers of mud. The layers

of mud prevent air from reaching the organic material and the resulting heat and increased pressure causes oil and gas to be formed. Oil is formed first and then as the temperature and the pressure increases gas begins to form.

Though petroleum and natural gas dominate Oman's economy, large deposits of copper, which supports a leading industry, have been discovered northwest of Muscat. The first evidence of copper production dated at Wadi Jizzi indicates that Oman has been a mineral producer for more than 5,000 years. Gold and silver are mined near Sohar. The mining industry is booming in Oman as new deposits of minerals are discovered.

The famous ophiolitic suite of rocks in Oman's mountains, provide copper, gold, silver, chromite and some lead, zinc and manganese. Exploration work is already under way by a number of companies for copper, and others for copper and gold. In the category of non-metallic minerals, huge commercial deposits of limestone, dolomite, silica sand/quartzite, various clays including kaolin and attapulgite, gypsum, marble, construction material in the form of aggregate and armour rocks, and low grade iron ore (laterite) and coal are also to be found.

Minerals such as those mentioned above are mined by specialists in their field but as amateurs we can take advantage of Oman's geology by collecting geodes which can easily be found in wadi beds and in some surface rock formations. Sometimes these geodes can be as big as footballs but it is more common to find geodes the size of tennis balls. Geodes are surprisingly light when picked up and that is because inside they are not solid rock and when cut open reveal a shell of crystals or agate, which are very beautiful. These are highly collectable and some people even insert small light bulbs and illuminate the crystals, which causes them to shine like diamonds.

Oman's Healing Springs

The natural springs of Oman are numerous and varied.

Not only do they provide water for domestic and agricultural use but many are known locally for their healing properties. There are hot and cold springs, mineral springs and fresh water springs suitable for drinking. Sulphur springs are best known for their healing properties for those who suffer from rheumatism, arthritis and any other pain associated with bones and joints. There are sulphur springs at Rustaq called Ain Al Kasfa. In Madha there are hot and cold springs used for curing skin ailments. These springs are hot in the winter and cold in the summer. Bausher a short distance from Muscat has hot mineral springs. There are hot springs at Rustaq and Nahkl, while Ain Razat in Salalah is notable for its crystal-clear cold springs which attract picnicking families throughout the year.

In Nakhal not far from the fort is the Al Thowrah hot springs this is a popular picnic area for tourists and locals. The spring originates in Jebal Nakhal and flows into a pool at the site. From here it trickles over a weir to the wadi floor and provides sustenance to the village. Children frolic in the pool and run barefoot across the wadi. The word Al Thowrah means boiling – the waters of the spring are not boiling hot, but pleasantly warm all year round. The people of Nakhal are proud of their spring, and live by an Omani proverb which "*Live near water and ask not about sustenance.*" They take the tourists in their stride and go on with their daily chores, a must really as Fridays and public holidays the roads to the spring at packed with parked cars.

One thoughtful tour operator posts the following on their website about Oman:-

After a hard-day's wandering an ancient site, trekking or exploring a new area there's no better way of relaxing than with a bath in a hot spring or mud bath. Allow the warm and often mineral-soaked waters and mud to work their magic on tired muscles and joints, soothing away aches and pains.

Royal Botanic Gardens

In 2006 when the Oman Botanic Gardens was established by Royal Decree, Oman once again became a leader in the Arabian world, with the largest Botanic Garden in the region, covering an area of 420 hectares. The Oman Botanic Garden has the world's largest collection of Arabian plants housed in the nursery section.

Oman is home to over 1,200 species of plants with 79 species found nowhere else in the world. Over the centuries Oman's plants have been used for medicinal purposes, perfumes, dyes, and crafts, beauty treatments, as animal fodder and to build homes. Frankincense and dates have been transported along trade routes and over oceans to provide for the empires of Rome, Egypt and Greece.

Sadly over 20% of these plants are threatened by environmental issues, due to habitat development, damage, over- grazing, climate change and even the modernization and construction of roads.

In the Oman Botanic Gardens a haven is being constructed to offer conservation and protection to the plants. Here is an opportunity to teach the new generations about plants and their needs, to educate young and old alike about the need to care for the environment and inform them that plants have provided for Omanis for thousands of years.

When the construction work is completed, The Oman Botanic Gardens will have, research laboratories, administration buildings, an amphitheater, exhibitions, shops and restaurants. There will be classrooms; accommodation blocks for students a seed bank and a library. The aim of the project is to conserve the biodiversity of Oman, through conservation and research. It will become a model for sustainability in the country as well as in the region, minimizing water waste. All waste will be treated on site and reused to irrigate the plants.

The aim of the project is to conserve the biodiversity of Oman, through conservation and research. It will become a model for sustainability in the country as well as in the region, minimizing water was. All waste will be treated on site and reused to irrigate the plants.

Once the whole garden is completed, visitors will be able to explore fog forests, baking sand desert, unique juniper forest, arid, salty sabkha, dry gravel desert and beautiful wadis all in one day, through the naturalistic habitats created on site. Impressive indoor 'biomes' will allow the climate to be carefully controlled, providing homes for plants from the southern Khareef to the northern mountains and Musandam.

The Oman Botanic Garden is located in Al Khoudh beyond the Sultan Qaboos University Hospital. As it is still under construction (2011) the garden is not yet open to the public, but more information can be found on their website www.omanbotanicgarden.com

Places of interest - Oman's Museums

Oman values its history and culture and Omani's believe that their heritage is important to their future development.

All aspects of Oman's history and culture are displayed in its many museums and play their part in enriching everyone's understanding of the past and the culture of Oman. Every museum is worth a visit and in most cases entrance is free or there is a very minimal charge. Take time to visit at least some of them. Even the children's museum is worth a visit by adults as it is very educational and great fun.

The Natural History Museum in Al Khuwair in the grounds of the Ministry of Heritage and Culture has fabulous displays of the wild life, flora and fauna of Oman as well as information on geology and fossils. The entrance to the museum has a fossilized tree that is 260,000,000 years old! In the same compound is the recently opened Sayyid Faisal bin Ali Museum, which was opened in 2008 and contains a collection of traditional weapons used in the country from the Stone Age to the 20th century.

The Children's Science Museum is located between Qurum and Medinat Qaboos. The Museum is housed in 2 dome shaped buildings clearly visible from the main highway. As previously stated this is a hands-on museum where the exhibits are update regularly and demonstrates science, inventions and discoveries in simplified methods. It is great fun for all ages.

Children's Science Museum

The National Museum in Ruwi is possibly one of the oldest museums in Oman and contains a letter which is said to be from the Prophet Mohammed sent to the two kings of Oman Abd and Jaifar in the 8th year of Hijra or 630 AD. There are also many artifacts, paintings and collections of items from the old Al Alam Palace in Muscat. The museum also has the Omani flag that was carried by Apollo 11 to the moon in 1969. This was an earlier design of the flag; the present Omani flag was carried to the moon by Apollo 17 in 1972. Some moon rocks were brought back to earth and these are on display in the museum.

The Bait Al Baranda Visitors Centre on the corniche in Muttrah is an art gallery and museum in one. It is a beautifully restored Omani home which was at one time home to the British Council and is well worth a visit. It regularly exhibits works of art, provides a venue for book launch parties, cultural events and is also a very well arranged museum with some fascinating displays and exhibits. Children will love the dinosaur, but don't be afraid if you hear a scream!

Muscat Gate Museum is located in the city walls and is a bit of a novelty in that the main road in and out of Muscat runs beneath the museum. If visiting Muscat this is an essential part of the tour.

Muscat Gate Museum

Bait Al Zubair in Muscat is a fabulous museum and is a must for all visitors to the region. This is a privately owned museum and houses a wonderful collection of weaponry, costumes, jewellery, photographs and documents that are part of a private collection. There are life size models of traditional mountain village houses, a town house, a falaj system, a barasti hut and a fishing boat. It also has at this time a wonderful display of Arabian Oryx in the grounds. These have been painted and decorated as part of a special exhibition amd have now found their home at Bait Al Zubair. There is also a miniture village scene complete with houses and residents.

Decorative Oryx on display in the grounds of Bait Al Zubair Museum

Detailed miniature villages in the grounds of Bait Al Zubair Museum

Omani national costumes on show in Bait Al Zubair Museum

Omani jewellery and burka's displayed in Bait Al Zubair Museum

The Sultan's Armed Forces Museum in Ruwi is a treasure trove of facts and interesting displays that will fascinate young and old alike. The museum is actually housed in what was originally Sultan Said Bin Sultan's summer house which was built in 1854. It later became the Garrison Headquarters. In 1900 it became the royal residence of Sultan Faisal bin Turkey but it was restored in 1988 by Sultan Qaboos as the Armed Forces Museum. There are displays of tanks and vehicles, models of a military first aid post, command centre, camouflage dugouts and even a bullet proof car used by the former Sultan. You definitely do not need a military background to enjoy a visit to this museum, but it may well whet your appetite for more information.

Bait Al Fransa is the Omani French Museum in Muscat. This was originally the residence of the French Consulate and was turned into a museum in 1992 following a visit made by His Majesty Sultan Qaboos to France in 1989. As a result it was decided that this historic building should be dedicated to the strong relationships between Oman and France.

Outside Muscat there are museums in Salalah, Sohar, Nakhl and Sur.
The Land of Frankincense Museum in Salalah is situated at Al Baleed Archaeological Park, a UNESCO World Heritage site, and houses two exhibitions. One for all things related to the history of frankincense and the other the maritime history of the region. The museum has a multi media room, coffee shop, souvenir shop and electric cars are available to help visitors to cover the whole site.

In Sur there is a Maritime Museum and there is soon to be a Fattah al Khair museum dedicated to the skill of the craftsmen making the traditional boats built at Sur.
Nakhl Fort Museum has a fine display of historic arms and weaponry from the 17th century to the present.

The Sohar Fort Museum tells the city's story from early Islam to the present, focusing on architecture and archaeology and the role played by Omani's in spreading the message of Islam to the rest of the world.

Nakhal Fort

Oman in the Guinness Book of Records

On the 23rd of July 2010 Oman celebrated its 40th Renaissance Day, the day on which His Majesty Sultan Qaboos came to power and ascended the throne. This time of national pride is celebrated by Government and citizens alike. As the 40th year of His majesty's reign was viewed as a landmark, many citizens were motivated to try to do something really special. National Day celebrated on the 18th of November (His Majesty's birthday) provided another opportunity for many to attempt to break world records in celebration of this 40th year.

The world's longest woven mat

Among the first to gain entry to the Guinness Book of Records on the 15th July 2010, was an entry from the Ladies of the Omani Woman's Association in Shinas who presented their woven mat made from palm leaves. It was the longest ever made and when completed the mat measured 38.5 meters and took 4 months to complete.

Oman once again entered the Guinness Book of World Records when 40 young Omani chefs prepared the world's largest Kabsa or Chicken Biriyani. At the Exhibition Centre at Seeb, the cooking pot was assembled, 4mts wide and 1.2 mts deep, and into it were placed 4000 kgs of rice and chicken, 2000 ltrs of cooking oil, 1000 kgs of vegetables and 100 kgs each of salt, spices and nuts. It took 10 hours to cook and an estimated

The world's largest Kabsa (chicken biriyani)

Shahim, holder of the 2009 record for the largest collection of car number plates.

70,000 people were fed with this Kabsa. The Kabsa was given to the needy and was distributed by charitable organisations to those attending Friday prayers at 5 of the cities Mosques, to prisoners and to those residents who attended the Exhibition Centre on Friday 23rd July.

In February 2011 another world record for Oman was set when a marble portrait of His Majesty Sultan Qaboos was found to be the largest in the world at 8 x 5 mts. The portrait, a mosaic of marble tiles made entirely of stones collected from within Oman all 128,274 of them, took 4 months to complete and is the work of Indian born Kasika Dewan, founder of Ka Design Atelier. The portrait was presented to His Majesty Sultan Qaboos on the occasion of the 40th National Day.

The 40th National Day was the inspiration for yet another world record. Risalati, the initiative of Haifa Mahmood Ali Suleiman, is a letter to His Majesty Sultan Qaboos. The first and longest letter written by the women of a nation in support of the Head of State showing their unconditional support of, and gratitude to, His Majesty the Sultan. Written by different races, faiths and nationalities the letter is representative of those women living and working in Oman at the time of the 40th National day in November 2010. When completed the letter weighed 375 kgs and was 2 kms long and 1.25 mts wide.

Earlier records set by Omanis or expatriates living in Oman include the following.
In May 2009, Shahin Ebrahim Mohajer, a Persian living in Oman, received his certificate from the Guinness Book of World Records as the holder of the largest collection of vehicle registration/ licence plates. Shahin from Muscat started to collect registration plates when we was 12 and now has a total of 561 different plates from all over the world.

In August 2009, Omar Al Mamari, aged 36, became the first Omani citizen to enter the GBR when he drove his Honda CBR 1100 bike from Oman's Automobile Association premises in Muscat to Salalah and returned back by the same route averaging a speed of 94.1 km. He covered a total distance of 2127 kms in 24-hours setting the world record for the greatest distance covered by an individual on a motorcycle in 24 hours.

SEA OF OMAN
Shinas
Liwa
Mahadah
Sohar
Saham
Al Khaburah
As S
Barka
As Seeb
MUSCAT
Bawshar
Wadi Al Maawil
Ar Rustaq
Nakhal
Bidbid
Samail
Al Awabi
Ibri
Al Hamra
Bahla
Nizwa
Izki
Manah
Dama
Taiyyin
Al Mudaybi
Adam
Bidiyyah

List of Contents

The Regions

Muscat 109

Al Batinah 119

Ad Dhakiliya 127

Adh Dhahirah 137

Dhofar 145

Musandam 155

Ash Sharqiyah 161

Al Buraimi 173

Al Wusta 177

Fables

Beauty and the snake 117

The frozen dates 125

The precious herb 134

The besieged brother 134

The bewitched girl 135

Zahrah 143

The solid ghee 153

The man who could see water 159

Burooj Kibaykib 169

Majlis al Jinn 170

The house of gold 171

Dancing with fire 180

MUSCAT GOVERNORATE

Muscat

The region of Muscat stretches from the capital area southeast to just beyond Qurayyat and northwest to Barka. The interior boundary is Rusail at the foothills of the mountains.

Muscat is the most densely populated of the regions in Oman with approximately, 775,878 people living in the region. Seeb is the most densly populated wilayat of the region with a population of over 300,000. The old city of Muscat is the political capital of the country and is filled with modern buildings and traditional houses that blend well together. More recent development and progress has caused the satellite towns of Al Khuwair, Medinat Al Sultan Qaboos, Al Ghubra and Al Qurum to be built.

All are within a very short distance from the beautiful white sandy beaches that help to make Oman such a wonderful tourist resort. Rugged mountains and wadis form a natural backdrop to add another dimension to the region.

Muscat became the capital in 1793 AD but archaeological evidence suggests that it was founded almost 900 years before that. The word Muscat means "anchorage" and the Al Alam Palace of H.M. Sultan Qaboos stands at the head of a natural deep-water harbour, guarded on either side by the twin forts of Mirani and Jelali.

In the 16th centuy, the Portuguese invaded Muscat and used it as their base for controlling the trade routes to India. Today Muscat is a bustling modern city, so it is hard to imagine that in 1970 there was only one sealed road in Muscat and the city gates were closed at sunset. Today most people refer to Muscat as the jewel of Arabia. Progress, development and modernisation have not affected Islamic values, tradition and culture. It is a modern city where the old harmonises with the new.

Things to see in Muscat.

Bait al Zubair is a wonderful museum that has all of the usual artifacts and photographs as well as reconstructions of an old Omani town house, a falaj system, a burasti house and mountain village house. This museum is an absolute delight and well worth a visit. Bait al Faransa and the National Museum should not be missed.

The old city gates, Bab al Kabir, the main gate, the Bab al Saghir, Bab al Mathaeeb and Bab al Waljat have all been restored, as have some of the clay walls.

The corniche from Muttrah to Muscat is a historic delight leading to the treasures of the souq, the fish market, Riyam Park, Kalbuh Park and then into Muscat.

Al Alam Palace Muscat

In the old city of Muscat, a visit to the Al Alam Palace is a must. This is one of the palaces of H.M. Sultan Qaboos. Nearby, the twin forts of Mirani and Jelali, once a prison and now a museum, though it is not often open to the public, stand guard over the capital.

Just beyond Muscat, there are the fishing villages of Sidab and Haramel, the Yacht Club, Marina and the Marine Science and Fisheries Centre. Continuing along the coast is the village of Al Bustan and the magnificent Al Bustan Palace Hotel. The hotel was built in 1985 for the Gulf Cooperation Council Meeting and is set in a private bay, surrounded on three sides by mountains and on the fourth side by the sea. The dhow, Sohar, built by Tim Severin, a British explorer who sailed to China to re-create the Sindbad voyage, marks the entrance to the hotel.

A spectacular drive over the mountain road to Bandar Jissa will bring you to a beautiful cove, ideal for swimming and picnics. Just around the next cove is the Oman Dive Centre.

Returning over the mountain road, Wadi Khabir and Ruwi are only a short distance away. Ruwi has lots of places to eat and shop. Ruwi High Street used to be the commercial

The Al Bustan Palace Hotel with the 'Sohar' in the foreground

centre of Oman, but new shopping centres and malls have redirected shoppers to out-of-town sites. The Armed Forces Museum at Bait Al Falaj is a fascinating and very well laid out museum for young and old alike.

Qurum has a wonderful park and rose garden and a number of shopping malls. Close by is the Oil Exhibition Centre and the Planetarium.

Just beyond Qurum on the way to Medinat Al Sultan Qaboos and Al Khuwair you will find the Children's Museum, and a little further up the road the Natural History Museum: a wonderful display of insects, animals, fossils, shells and rocks. History begins even before you enter the door, as there is a fossilised tree outside the main entrance that is two hundred and sixty million years old!

Two of the many cruise liners now a common sight in Muscat harbour

Coffee pots, a symbol of Omani hospitality , on a roundabout near Bustan

A tribute to Oman's historical heritage, this mock fort on the rock face at Darsait

FABLE Beauty and the snake

Long ago in the village of Bausher, very near Muscat, lived a very beautiful woman. Each evening at 6 o'clock, when she went to wash in the falaj, a snake would appear. The snake would coil itself around her body so that she became paralysed and quite unable to move.

One day she decided that though her husband was a very jealous man, she must tell him about the snake. Her husband was very angry and decided to take his gun and go to the falaj with his wife and hide until the snake appeared. As soon as the snake began to approach his wife the man shot at the snake, but the snake and his wife disappeared!

He was so upset that he went to the local religious man, the Alim, and asked for his advice. The Alim gave the man a letter and told him to go to Wadi Al Ghail behind the hot springs, wait there and give the letter to the first person or thing that approached him.

A dog was the first thing to approach him on the third night after his wife had disappeared, so he gave the letter to the dog. The dog immediately started to walk backwards to indicate that he wanted the man to follow him.

They arrived at what looked like a deserted cave, but as the man went deeper inside he saw that it was full of ancient people.

An old man took the letter and told the man that he had shot his son. The snake had been the son of a jinn and then the man realised that all the ancient people in the cave were jinns. He told the old man that he only tried to kill a snake. The old man told him never to kill snake again, because a snake may not always be a snake! The man left the cave and returned to his home determined never to kill a snake again and when he arrived home, he was overjoyed to find his wife waiting for him.

(Sultanate of Oman)
AL BATINAH REGION
SEA OF
OMAN
Shinas
Liwa
Mahadah
Sohar
l Buraymi
Saham
Al Khaburah
AL BATINAH
REGION
As Suwayq
Al Musanaah
Bar
ynah
Dank
Yanqul
Ar Rustaq
Nakh
Samail
Al Awabi
Ibri
Al Hamra
Bahla
Nizwa
Izki
Manah
Adam

Al Batinah

The Batinah region is the coastal plain that stretches north of the Muscat region almost up to the border with the United Arab Emirates, a distance of almost 270 kms and spreads inland to the Western Hajar Mountains. It has the second largest percentage of the population after Muscat with 772,590 people living in its 12 wilayats.

The Batinah region is one of Oman's most important geographical and economic locations, and has always been Oman's main maritime and trading centre. It is often referred to as the belly of the country, as the word Batinah means front or inner. The Western Hajar Mountains run parallel to the coastline and the rains from the mountain range mean that the soil is fertile and rich in minerals. This enables date palms to flourish and bananas and fruits to grow. The sea provides excellent fishing opportunities, so the main occupations are either farming or fishing.

The main town on the coast is Sohar, which has a long-established history of mining copper, and a maritime trading link with India and the Far East. Historical documents tell us that Sohar was once known as Magan and once exported copper to Mesopotamia. Trading in earlier days included a wide variety of goods including beeswax, figs, dates, pomegranates, bananas, ivory and tortoiseshell. One of the most famous sailors and traders believed to have been born in Sohar is Sindbad the Sailor, made famous for his exploits in the 1001 Arabian Nights.

The British Explorer Tim Severin re-

created one of Sindbad's voyages when he sailed to Canton in China in 1980 in a handmade dhow. In the 16th and 17th centuries, the Portuguese believed that Sohar was the most important city for their control over the Arabian Sea, but their attempt to capture the city failed. Today Sohar has a much smaller population than it had as far back as the 10th century when it was a very prosperous town. Before Islam, the Portuguese occupied Sohar many times.

Sohar fort, with its five round towers and one square tower was built in the reign of the Prince of Hormuz, Baha Al Din Ayadh, which lasted from 1294 to 1312. He must have been afraid of invading forces because he built an escape tunnel under the fort that is 10 kms long. Modern day Sohar is the home of a prosperous industrial estate, many of the industries having attracted foreign investment to the region and Oman.

The coastal plain of the Batinah region has some wonderful beaches and fishing villages, where in the correct season around April and May you will see locally caught

sardines drying in the sun on the beach. If you get there early enough you will see the local fisherman landing their catch and sometimes selling this to villagers and tourists.

Suwaiq was once a very active port like Sohar and Barka and has a fort facing the beach. Other villages of interest are Barka, Al Khaboura and Al Sawadi, often called the shell beach, because of the large number of shells that are washed up on it.

Khutmat Milaha, Wadi Jizzi and Wadi Hatta are the checkpoints for entry by road into United Arab Emirates.

In the inland region, Rustaq and Nakhl are two of the most important towns.

Rugged mountains, wadis and fertile plantations create a spectacular backdrop to the towns and villages in the area. Rustaq was once the capital of the region and still has the administrative offices for the ministries, a main hospital and two colleges. There are hot springs that are believed to have medicinal properties and people come to the region to be cured of their ailments. Rustaq fort is very nice indeed and has four towers. It has been built and restored several times since the original building in the 7th century. Near to the springs at Rustaq are the remains of the house and clinic of one of the most famous doctors in the 15th century. Rashid Bin Umaira Bin Thani was born in Rustaq at the end of the 15th century and was highly educated.

The Ministry of National Heritage and Culture stores his manuscripts and writings and some are in the private library of Sayyid Mohammad Bin Ahmed in Seeb. He wrote about traditional Omani medicine, offered techniques and cures, many of which are similar to those still used today. His most famous work offers a remedy for all illnesses known at the time and includes the anatomy of the eye, heart disease and psychological disorders. He even documented surgical procedures to cure breast cancer. Many of his writings are in the form of poems to help with memorisation of the information.

Nakhl, too, has a fort which is over three hundred and fifty years old, and like that of Rustaq has played an important part in Oman's history. The word Nakhl means date palms, and because of the rich fertile soil in the region there are a great many date plantations. Like Rustaq there are hot springs believed to have healing properties.

Because of the mountains and the wadis, the area around Rustaq and Nakhl has become very popular with tourists and local residents who like to go *wadi bashing*. Wadi bashing is a sport or leisure-time pursuit that has been created since four-wheel-drive cars and trucks were introduced. It involves finding a dry riverbed and bumping over

Nakhl fort

rough roads and rocks left behind in the riverbed in a four-wheel-drive, to search for a place to picnic. If you are lucky and find a wadi that still has a pool or is still flowing then a swim is essential.

Some of the most famous wadis are Wadi Bani Kharus, Bilad Sayt, Wadi Bani Auf and Snake Gorge. At Wadi Bani Kharus, it is possible to see sea fossils and rock drawings that are said to be fifteen hundred years old. The limestone rocks are somewhere between ninety million and two hundred and eighty million years old, and if you go further into the wadi you will find rocks that are six hundred million years old. The Ghamama Mosque, one of the oldest mosques in Oman, is also in the Wadi Bani Kharus region.

In Mahsanah, there are houses with ornate windows that are built in the style of those found in Yemen.

To reach Snake Gorge you need to go to Wadi Bani Auf first. There is a lot of natural quartz in this area that can easily been seen on the bed of the wadi. Snake Gorge is very, very deep and it can be very dangerous to try to go through. There are high boulders, very deep pools and sometimes sudden winds in the gorge can whip up the water making it very dangerous. It sounds exciting and beautiful but it is dangerous and no one should ever attempt to go into the gorge without a guide and certainly never alone. If it is raining flash floods can bring disaster. Bilad Sayt is one of the most picturesque villages in the region as the mountains offer stunning views of the gorge and the villages below.

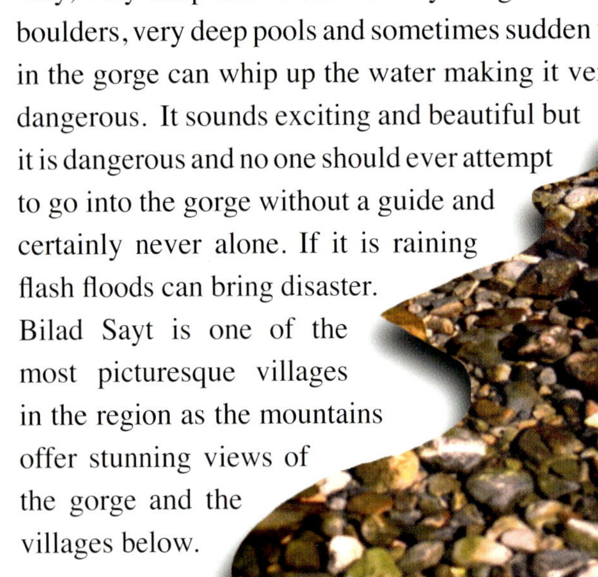

FABLE The frozen dates

Once upon a time, in Nakhl, there lived a wise, wealthy and generous Imam. One day a "shawii", a shepherd from a village in Wadi Mistel, came to see the Imam to ask him if he could store a sack of dates in his storeroom until the next winter. The shepherd only had very poor quality or "Naghal" dates, but because he was a poor shepherd, the dates were very important to him.

The Imam asked the shepherd to write his name on the sack of dates so that he would be able to find them when he wanted them. When winter came the shepherd returned to the Imam and asked if he could go to the storeroom to collect his sack of dates. The kind and generous Imam told the shepherd that he could collect his dates anytime. When he entered the storeroom the shepherd found lots and lots of sacks of very good quality dates called "fardh" dates and his own little sack of poor quality "naghal" dates. The poor shepherd could not resist the temptation! He took a bag of good quality "fardh"dates instead of his own poor "naghal" dates.

He split the sack into two portions and put them on the back of his donkey and left the Imam's storeroom as quickly as he could to return to his village. When the Imam went to the storeroom to get some of his own "fardh" dates, he was shocked and surprised to see the sack of "naghal "dates with the shepherd's name on it. He asked the guard if the shepherd had been to collect his dates and when the guard said yes, the Imam realized what the shepherd had done.

Because the Imam was a kind and generous man, he said, "If the shepherd has taken my dates by mistake, may he enjoy them, but if he intended to steal my dates, may they turn to stone!"

If you go to Wadi Mistel, you can still see the sack split into two large stones where they fell off the donkey's back!

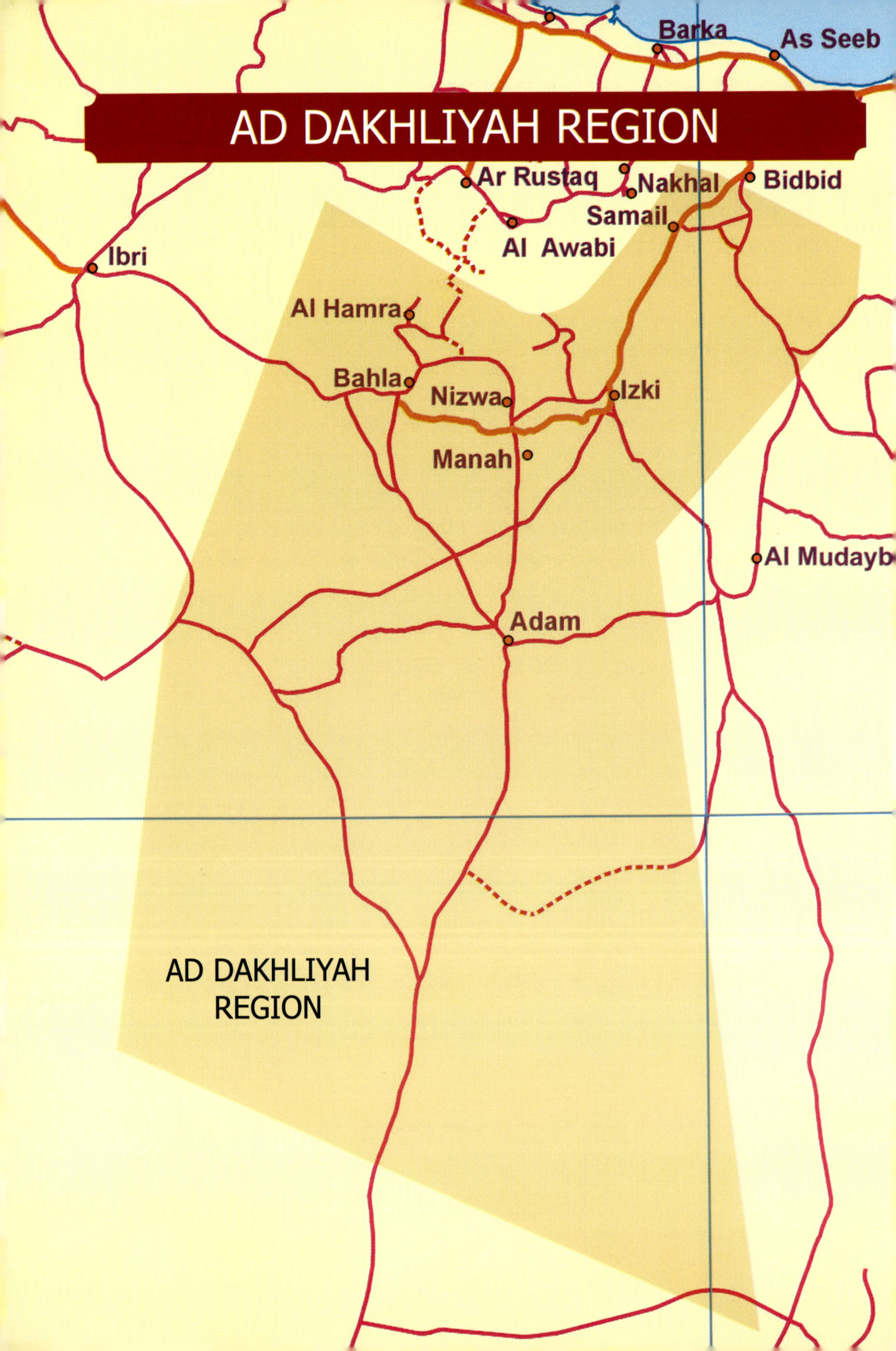
AD DAKHLIYAH REGION
Barka
As Seeb
Ar Rustaq
Nakhal
Bidbid
Samail
Al Awabi
Ibri
Al Hamra
Bahla
Nizwa
Izki
Manah
Al Mudayb
Adam
AD DAKHLIYAH REGION

Ad Dakhliyah

The interior region of Dakhiliyah links Muscat and the coastal regions with the rest of Oman. The Sumail Gap in the Hajar Mountains is the natural crossing point from east to west and vice versa.

Dakhiliyah has 8 wilayats and a population of 326,651 and is the staging post, the pivotal link between the different regions of the Sultanate.

The importance that Sumail has played in the history of Oman is evident by the number of forts and watchtowers that line the old trading routes. The region is steeped in history. The first Omani to embrace Islam was from Sumail. Mazin Bin Ghaduba made the pilgrimage to meet the Prophet Mohammed. The ancient capital of Oman, Nizwa, is in the Dakhiliyah region and the famous "Green Mountain" or Jebal Akhdar is a major tourist attraction in the region.

The Dakhiliyah region extends from Fanja to Adam and passes through Izki and Manah, and in the western Hajar to Nizwa and Bahla.

The fort at Nizwa dates back to the 17th century and is considered a very important historical site. Nizwa is the birthplace of many poets, writers and intellectuals.

Nizwa was the political and cultural capital of Oman from the 2nd century Hijra (after the birth of Mohammed - approximately 800 – 900 AD). At that time the Imams or religious leaders were the rulers and Imam Sultan Bin Saif Bin Malik Al Ya'arubi built a magnificent fort at Nizwa. The fort took many years to build but was completed in 1668. The fort is the core of the town of Nizwa. There is a souq nearby where traditional craftsman can be seen working with silver, making jewellery and khanjars, weaving and making pots. The craftsmen of the Nizwa area are some of the finest in the country and their skills as silversmiths are legendary. The souq, once made up of hundreds of dark little alleyways, has been restored and renovated so it is much more modern, but still has lots of charm.

Architects and builders were very busy in Nizwa in the 2nd century Hijra. The mosque, which stands in the centre of the city next to the fort, was built at the same time as the fort. The mosque, called at the time the *Imam's Mosque*, was reconstructed in 1970 and renamed the Sultan Qaboos Mosque.

Bahla fort before the restoration

There are a number of small mosques and tombs positioned just outside the city. Perhaps the most famous is the tomb and mosque of Warith Bin Ka'ab, an Imam who came to live in Nizwa to restore justice around 179 Hijra. He died while trying to save some prisoners that he had imprisoned in a small cell in the wadi. The wadi flooded and the prisoners and the Imam and his guards all drowned. He was buried beside the wadi were he died and a small mosque has been erected in his memory.

There are some typical Omani graveyards on either side of the road and one has the oldest tombs and graves in Nizwa. Some of these are for the Imams and scholars who shaped the history and culture of Oman. There are many picturesque and interesting small towns and villages in the area around Nizwa.

Villages like Fanja, Bidbid, Sumail, Manal, Izki and Birkat Al Mawz, are all worth a visit.

Birkat Al Maws, which means *banana pools*, is on the way to the famous Jebal Akhdar, about which we will hear more later. At Izki, you can visit the cave of Jarnan where legend tells us there is a golden calf. The people of Izki worshiped the calf before Islam came to Oman, when they then hid the calf in the cave.

The villagers of Izki love to tell the story of the Sufi woman who used one of the mountain caves to worship God. One day a wild animal that looked like a lion attacked her. Because of her strong faith in God, God froze the lion in the air as she prayed for help. The remains of the lion in the form of a rock can still be seen today.

If you are going to Nizwa from Sumail, as you pass through Manal near Wadi Halfayn test your fitness by climbing the *Persian Steps*. There are 1,400 steps cut into the cliff! It takes about two hours to climb to the top. No one actually knows why these are called the Persian Steps, but Omanis do have a habit of calling anything that is very old, Persian.

Jebal Akhdar, the famous Green Mountain, is well known for its beautiful roses. At the top of the Jebal is the Saiq plateau, and Saiq, which is the highest town in Oman.

The villages all have terraces of fruit trees: almonds, pomegranates, apples, peaches and cherries, and garlic. The farmers of Jebal Akhdar are famous for their roses and the rosewater that they distil. The rosewater is used in cooking as perfume and even added to coffee. At the end of a meal, which is eaten with the fingers, rosewater from a special silver rosewater sprinkler is used to clean and freshen the hands.

The founder of the Al Busaidi dynasty was born in Adam. The mosque named after him and his residence can be found in Harrat Al Jamie. Adam has a very interesting history dating back to pre–Islamic times and several archaeological sites have been found. There are mosques, citadels, forts and deserted souqs. It is the last green oasis before entering the desert. Villagers in Adam tell the story of the "built by itself mosque" or Masjid Bani Ruhuh.

Unable to decide on the style of the mosque that they wanted to build, after discussing and arguing long into the night, they went to sleep. In the morning when they woke up, the mosque had been built, as if by magic!

The deserted village of Tanuf, which was destroyed in the Jebal Wars in the 1950s, can be found beyond Nizwa town centre. The natural spring that provides a popular mineral water *Tanuf* is also in this area. The original falaj system still flows through the village and along the cliffs. One of Oman's most famous caves, Al Hoti cave (pronounced Al Hoota) is near the main Nizwa to Bahla

road. The cave has some of the most wonderful stalagmites and stalactites. If you are planning to visit the cave you should have an experienced guide with you.

Jebal Shams, or Sun Mountain, is actually the highest mountain in Oman reaching a height of three thousand metres. Wadi Ghul and Misfah are beautiful villages in the shadow of Jebal Shams. In the villages leading up to Jebal Shams, you will see villagers selling the red and black woollen rugs that are very common in the area. That is because the top of the mountain can be very cool, perhaps even cold, especially at night and so the villagers need rugs to help to keep warm.

Bahla, a small town near Nizwa, is very famous for its potters and pottery. A visit to the pottery is very interesting as you can watch the potters at work and visit the clay kilns. Bahla is also well known for jinns and magic. Omanis and tourists alike are fascinated by the tales of magic and sorcery that are told in the souqs and coffee shops in the area — tales that are passed down from father to son. There is even a story about a flying mosque! Who needs a flying carpet when you can have a flying mosque?

Legend tells us that the mosque was originally in Rustaq, but was moved overnight to the highest of the hills outside Bahla.

The fort at Bahla is thought to be one of the oldest in Oman and has been listed by UNESCO as an important heritage site. The fort was built in the 17th century and has recently been renovated. It has six towers and a wall that is twelve kms long. The wall has 15 gates and 132 watchtowers.

A short drive from Bahla is Jabrin Fort. It is possibly one of the best forts in Oman. It was built as the home of the Imam and is the burial place of Imam Bil'arab. Jabrin Fort was built in the mid-17th century and was restored in 1983. This fort has magnificent Islamic and floral patterns painted on its wooden ceilings and beams. There are false floors and secret passages and it even has its own Koran school in one of the upper rooms and a special room for the Imam's favourite horse! A visit to this fort is essential.

FABLE The precious herb

Long, long ago in a village right on the top of Jebal Akhdar, Oman's famous Green Mountain, a man became very ill. No one knew what was wrong with him or how to cure him. His family was so unhappy because no one could help him so they decided to travel to Medina to see the Holy Prophet Mohammed – peace be upon Him.

The Prophet Mohammed talked to the man and his family and asked where they had come from. When they answered that they had come all the way from Oman, the Prophet told them there was a plant growing on Jebal Akhdar and this would cure the man. All they had to do was boil the leaves, drink the juice, and God willing the man would be cured.

Happy and relieved that the cure was so simple the family left Medina to return home to Oman. As soon as they arrived in their village on the top of the Green Mountain, they went out and gathered the plant that the Prophet told them about.

The plant was thyme, an herb we use today in cookery and tea.
They boiled the leaves and gave the infusion to the man to drink. Slowly he began to feel stronger, but he was not completely cured. His family decided to go back to Medina and see the Prophet again. Anxious to know why the man had not been cured the Prophet asked to see the thyme.

When the thyme was brought to the Prophet, he asked the plant why it had not completely cured the man.

The plant replied saying, "I ask for your forgiveness. I have cured him of ninety-nine ailments, but I cannot save him from the one that remains - death."

FABLE The besieged brother

In the 17th century Imam Bil' Arab bin Sultan, a generous ruler and scholar, lived in Jabrin fort. The fort was built on sand and gravel plains, miles away from the nearest town of Bahla. This was quite an unusual setting for a fort, but the Imam liked solitude, peace and quiet. He opened a school in the fort and spent his life surrounded by artists, poets and philosophers. He was very interested in astronomy and had two rooms in the fort called the Sun room and the Moon room. The fort is famous for the delicate paintwork on the ceilings and intricate plasterwork.

Unfortunately Saif, who was Bil' Arab's brother fought with him for the leadership of the country. He declared himself to be the Imam even though Bil' Arab was still alive. One by one Saif took control of all of the fortified buildings in the area, until Bil' Arab was surrounded and trapped in Jabrin fort. Bil' Arab knew that his people were suffering and realised that he couldn't win. He prayed to God for deliverance and the next morning he was found dead! He lies buried inside Jabrin fort.

FABLE The bewitched girl

In ancient times, long, long ago when the jinns flew around on flying carpets, a young girl from Nizwa died. She was just nine years old. A few days after she died a shepherd was passing the place where she had been buried and saw that the tomb was empty.

Sometime later the girl's mother went to visit the Bedouin who lived on the edge of the village. In the village she saw her daughter playing with her friends and was very shocked. She ran up to the girl and said that she was her mother, but the girl didn't recognise her. A Bedouin woman had seen this and came up to the woman and told her to leave the girl alone because she was the mother of the girl. The two women began to quarrel and so they took their case to the judge.

The judge listened to both women as each explained that the girl was their daughter. The judge told both women to stay awake all night and the next morning they had to tell him about the planet Venus. The next morning both women came to tell the judge what they had seen.

The Bedouin explained that Venus moved from the far right to the far left of the moon. The other woman said, "By the name of Allah and His Prophet Mohammed, Your Honour, the planet hardly left its position near the moon."

The judge decided that the girl's true mother was the second woman as she had stayed up all night out of love for her daughter, while the Bedouin must have fallen asleep. The judge ordered that the girl should be given back to her real mother and they returned to their village happy again.

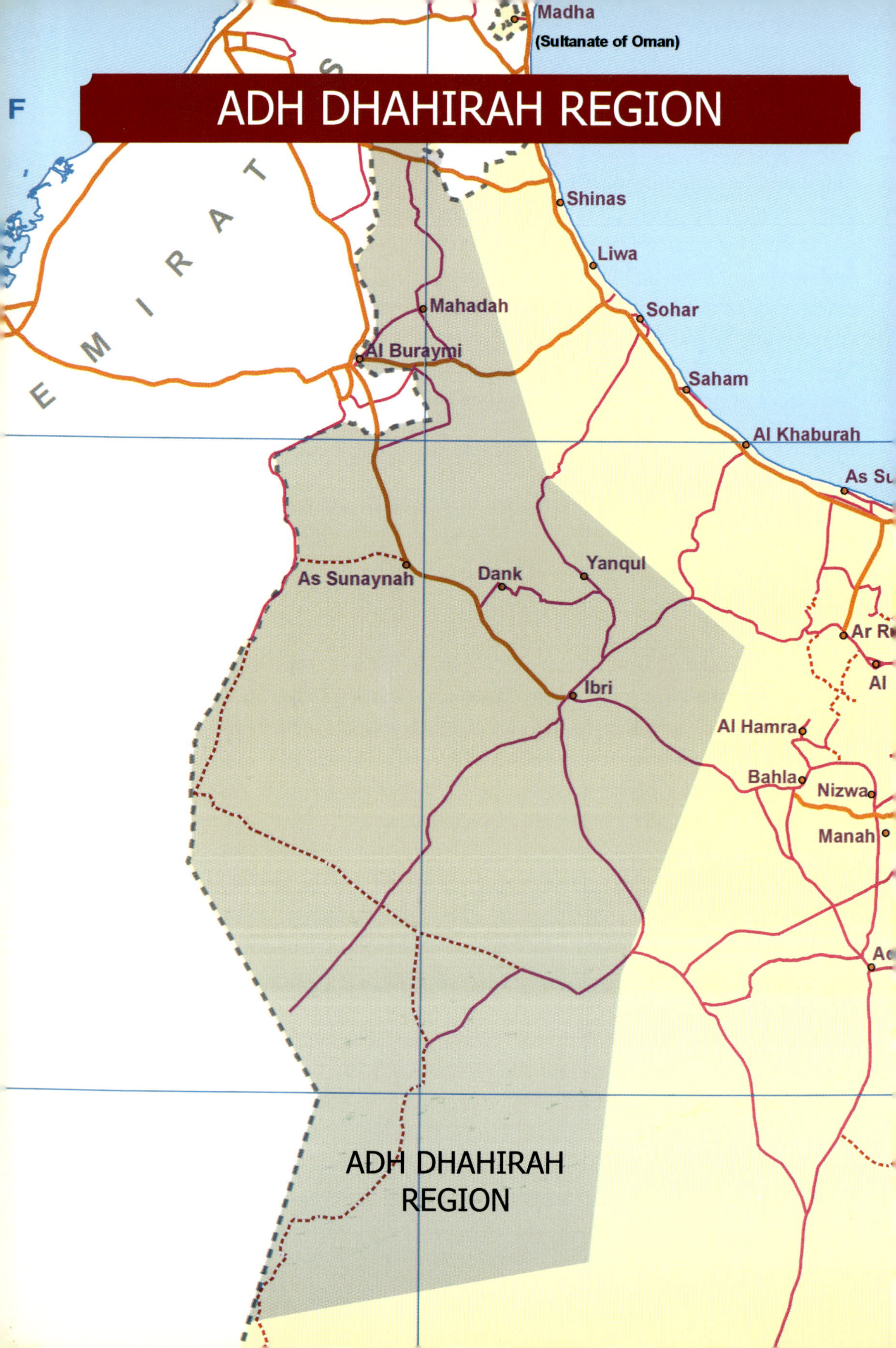
ADH DHAHIRAH REGION
Madha
(Sultanate of Oman)
F
E M I R A T E S
Shinas
Liwa
Sohar
Mahadah
Al Buraymi
Saham
Al Khaburah
Yanqul
Dank
As Sunaynah
Ibri
Al Hamra
Bahla
Nizwa
Manah
ADH DHAHIRAH
REGION

ADH Dhahirah

The back, or to give it its Arabic name, Adh Dhahirah is in the northwest of Oman. It stretches from the foothills of the western Hajar and continues to the Rub Al Khali or Empty Quarter. Adh Dhahirah has a population of just 151,669 in its 3 wilayats but has high levels of agricultural production and several oil and gas fields.

Ibri is the administrative capital and is the largest town in the Dhahirah region and the second largest wilayat in Oman. Other major towns are Dhank, Yanqul and Mahdhah. In the past camel trains of traders made their way through the area, but today oil is the great provider of wealth and work. Fahud is the most famous site in the Ibri region.

In 1963 Oman's first oil well produced oil and in 1966 a pipeline was laid from Fahud to Mina Al Fahal in Muscat. Fahud now produces one-third of Oman's oil.

Archaeological sites are also strategically important. There are a vast number of graves in Dhahirah that have encouraged UNESCO to list the region on its World Heritage List. In Bat there are traces of the Umn Al Nar civilization that is believed to have been from 2000–2700 BC and also the Hafit culture from 2500–3000 BC. These

Bat tombs with Jebal Shams behind

discoveries included communal graves and beehive tombs. Similar cultures have been found in the United Arab Emirates and in Saudi Arabia.

Those who are not engaged in oil production are farmers, weavers or craftsmen. Indigo dying used to be very important in this region but now only small quantities of the plant that produces the dye are grown. The traditional and distinctive rugs and blankets in black and red are woven in the Ibri region.

The Al Wadah falaj in the Bat region is well known because it stops and starts flowing every few days.

Local legend tells us that a snake lives in the falaj and even though it is a good snake or jinn, it blocks the flow of water with its body. When the villagers tell the snake that there is an emergency and they need water he moves his body and the water flows freely through the falaj. Quite close to this are the beehive tombs that have been dated back to 2500-3500 BC.

Yanqul's Jebal al Hawra dominates the town and in the past wolves, Tahr and gazelles used to roam over this mountain, but not anymore. Today Yanqul is the main crossing point between the Western Hajar and the Batinah region. The area has lots of forts and watchtowers. One of the oldest pre-Islamic forts is of great importance to Oman's history simply because it was at this strategic crossing point. The falaj of Al Ain runs through the fort. There are rich mineral deposits of copper and more recently gold and silver near Yanqul. Dhank is a very popular destination for visitors to the region. There are many watchtowers and forts, underground springs, aflaj and a wadi that always has water in it.

Mahdhah may be the smallest wilayat in the region, but it is the birthplace of the first Arab Ambassador to the United States of America as far back as 1840. He was Ambassador Ahmed Bin Nu'man Al Ka'abi.

FABLE Zahrah

Once upon a time, the village of Dank was suffering from a prolonged drought. The villagers prayed for rain but God did not seem to hear their prayers. The Sheik of the village called all the people together to ask them for their suggestions for the best way to get rain. One family thought that God would listen to the prayers of their daughter as she was the most beautiful girl in the village.

Everyone agreed, so they asked Zahrah to pray for them. God told Zahrah that he would send rain but there was a price to be paid. Zahrah would have to join him in the sky and become a new shining star. Zahrah wanted to help her village, so she agreed and it began to rain immediately. The people of Dank were very happy because rain would mean that their crops would grow and they would have a good harvest.

Every night when the people of Dank look into the sky and see the brightest star, they remember Zahrah, her beauty and the price she paid for rain to make her people happy.

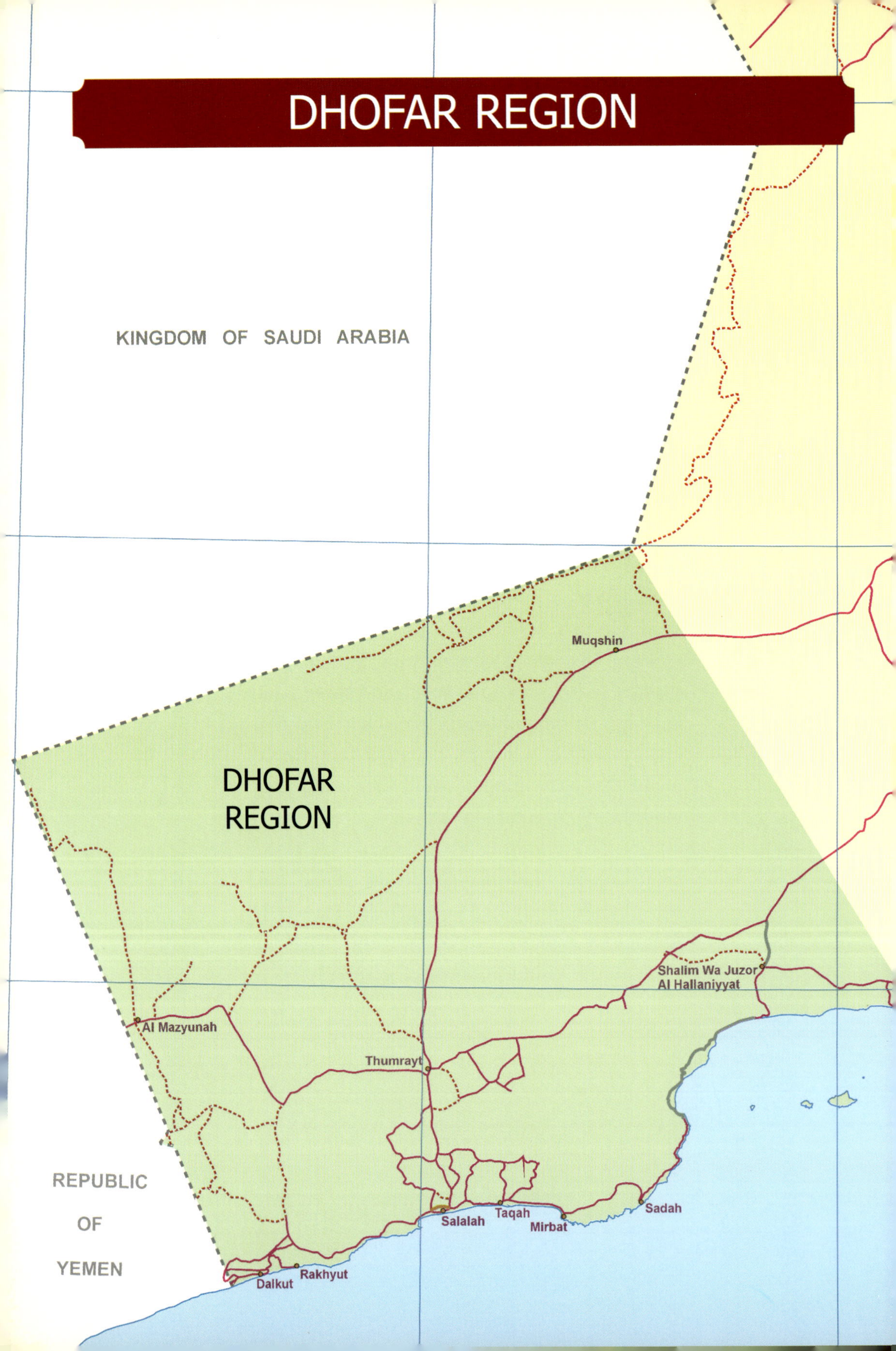

DHOFAR REGION
KINGDOM OF SAUDI ARABIA
DHOFAR
REGION
Muqshin
Shalim Wa Juzor
Al Hallaniyyat
Al Mazyunah
Thumrayt
REPUBLIC
OF
YEMEN
Salalah
Taqah
Mirbat
Sadah
Rakhyut
Dalkut

Dhofar Region

In the extreme south of the country bordering the Republic of Yemen is the Dhofar region of Oman. With its tropical climate and monsoon season, Dhofar is unlike any other region in Oman. Salalah is the capital of the region and is rapidly being developed into a modern commercial centre. At one time, before His Majesty the Sultan came to power, what we now know as the Sultanate of Oman was known as Muscat and Oman. (Oman being the southern region)

The Dhofar region is so very different from the rest of the country in terms of climate that it is easy to believe that it is another country. In the rest of the country we think of deserts and bare rocky mountains, but in Dhofar there are waterfalls, lush green slopes on the mountains and fertile soil that can easily support farms and agricultural projects. In the section on frankincense we have already mentioned the importance that this fragrance has in the region and in history. The poem by John Masefield entitled *Cargoes* begins: "*Quinquireme of Nineveh from distant Ophir ... With cargoes of emeralds and apes and peacocks, sandalwood, cedar wood and sweet white wine*."

Ophir is believed to be Dhofar and though Masefield doesn't actually say that the cargoes included frankincense, I am sure that it was part of that precious cargo. Traders as far back as 1,000 BC shipped frankincense from Dhofar to Egypt and Assyria. The Bible tells us that one of the gifts the wise men took to the baby Jesus was frankincense. The Song of Solomon talks about frankincense and the Queen of Sheba is known to have travelled to Dhofar to buy her frankincense. Steeped in history and the mists of the monsoon season, Dhofar is truly different from the rest of Oman.

Dhofar covers an area of 100,000 square kms and has a population of approximately 249,729 people living in 10 wilayats. Each year from June to September the monsoon season known as the Khareef, brings its mists and rain creating

waterfalls and humidity to give life to trees and plants that cover the whole area. During the Khareef season Salalah hosts a month long festival where thousands of tourists descend on the region from the neighbouring Gulf States and even from as far away as Europe to see the transformation that the Khareef brings. The whole area is rich in ancient history and there are often archeological teams working there. Perhaps one of the most famous is the team that believes it discovered the *lost city of Ubar*.

The region is divided into desert, coastal plains and mountains. The coastal plains attract many migrating birds. Agriculture thrives and there are numerous cattle farms and crops such as bananas, papaya, coconuts, and sugar cane etc. all of which are usually associated with tropical countries and not those of the Gulf States. Jebali people live in the mountains and many of the areas have been divided into tribal regions. Many of the Jebalis are herdsmen and often mountain caves become their homes when the weather is stormy. Jebalis have a very distinctive style of dress and do not wear the dishdasha that we have talked about in other regions. It is more common to see a wizar wrapped around the waist with a shirt on top, and the kumah is replaced with a turban style of headdress.

The Rub Al Khali or the Empty Quarter is the desert region of Dhofar and flows into the southern part of Saudi Arabia. The desert temperatures are fierce in the summertime, so the Duru tribes of desert people often move to Adam and Ibri to escape the heat. Water and vegetation is hard to find as many of the sand dunes are actually made up of salt washed down from the mountains in the rainy season and crusted by the sun over hundreds of years until it is several metres thick. Duru history tells us that children of the tribe were raised on camel or goats milk and did not taste water until they were ten years old.

Salalah is the main town in Dhofar and has all of the administrative buildings of Government as well as modern hospitals and schools, and it is home to the second major airport in Oman. The main industries are fishing, farming and agriculture, jewellery making, and now tourism especially in the Khareef season. Archeological remains show that between the 12th and 16th centuries, there was a magnificent city in the Haffa district of Salalah, where there is evidence of a mosque, palace, houses and tombs. In the Quran you will find the story of the 14 footprints of the Prophet's sacred camel. On the 23rd July Street the main street in Salalah you will find the 14 footprints embedded in the rock. These are now fenced off to protect them.

Verdant green pastures in Salalah after the Khareef monsoon

The Salalah Museum, part of the National Heritage and Culture Centre, contains some wonderful exhibits. Amongst them is the message sent by the Prophet Mohammed to Abd and Jaifer calling Oman to accept Islam as its true religion.

Just outside Salalah and to the north you will find Job's Tomb or to use the Arabic name, Nabi Ayoub. Near the tomb is a small mosque believed to have been used by Job for prayers. There are beautiful springs, streams, gardens and caves at Ain Razat and Ain Homran, which make ideal places for picnics.

Thumrayt is ideally placed to link Salalah with the rest of Oman as the main highway to the north of the country goes through it. In times gone by it used to be part of the caravan route for camel trains passing through the Arabian Peninsula. Frankincense trees were once found in great quantities in the Thumrayt area, but today there are not quite so many. The lost city of Ubar is in the Thumrayt region at Shisr and was rediscovered in 1992, as a result of images seen on American satellite pictures, and so the lost city was found.

After years of archeological digs had failed to locate the city, these satellite photos were used and they showed old caravan routes buried below the sand. With the help of the local Bedouin they eventually found the remains of walls, towers and gates, pottery, incense pots and glass which have been dated back to 100 BC.

East of Salalah is Taqah, where His Majesty the Sultan's mother is buried. Wadi Dharbat is a natural park with waterfalls, lakes and mountains. This region is an ideal place to see lots and lots of camels. In fact there are so many camels in the area that they are a danger to the natural vegetation and it was once thought that it would be best to sell some of the camels to other parts of the world such as Australia. In the Dharbat valley there are caves with stalagmites and stalactites.

Some caves have paintings which are believed to have been the rock art of the Jebali who used the caves as shelter. One of the caves in this region is thought to be one of the largest natural caves in Oman.

To visit the remains of the Queen of Sheba's Palace you will need to travel to Sumhuram. The Queen is reported to have built the palace so that she had somewhere to stay and rest when she came to Salalah from Yemen to buy her frankincense.

At Marbat, which was once the capital of Dhofar region, you will find the tomb of Bin Ali. Marbat was a famous port used for exporting fish and abalone. Abalone was once a source of pearls but is now a much-prized food in the Far East.

To the west of Salalah the container port and duty-free zone of Raysut has brought a lot of industry to the region and improved the work prospects for local citizens.

At Mughsayl, where the mountains meet the sea you will find blowholes. Walking over the rocks you can hear the sea under the rocks and when the tide is high the water bursts up through the holes in the rocks to form fountains.

The road from Salalah to the Yemeni border is one of the most spectacular in the country with hairpin bends that are almost terrifying, and yet the road itself is a wonderful feat of engineering. The views from the road as it winds around the mountain are amazing. A spectacular end to a spectacular part of the country.

FABLE The solid ghee

In the province of Dhofar in the South of Oman, and old man and his wife were making assidya, a savory dish which is famous in Salalah, when they realised that they did not have enough ghee.

The old woman scolded her husband, "Didn't you go to the souq this morning?"
"Yes, but I didn't have any money," he replied.

The assidya was getting cold and they needed more ghee, so they decided on a plan to go back to the souq and get some ghee.

The old man told his wife to put on a shawl and hide a small pot under it. As they approached the souq, he would pretend to beat her with a stick and she must pretend to cry.

"I wish there was another way to get some ghee?" said the old woman, but still she set off to the souq with her husband. Just before the entrance to the souq she began to scream and wail,

"You have tortured me and made my life a misery." A crowd soon gathered to see what all the noise was about.

"Why are you beating her?" asked some and others asked, "Why are you crying like that?"

"She is lazy, just sleeps all day and doesn't do any work," replied the old man.
"Then send her back to her family," shouted the crowd.
"No!" replied the man, "she must go home with me."
When they arrived at the door of the shop that sold the ghee, the old woman sat down and began to cry and shout,
"Help me, help me, this man is making my life a misery."
The shopkeeper felt sorry for the old lady so he took her inside the shop and asked her to sit down and wait while he tried to calm the old man down.

Once she was inside the shop, the old lady locked the door and began to hunt for the ghee. When she found it she was puzzled, because the ghee was solid and would not pour into the pot she had hidden under her shawl.

She didn't know what to do, so she shouted out to her husband,
"Be quiet out there, you son of the solid ghee!"
Her husband understood her message and shouted back,
"If you think I am the son of the solid ghee then I will have to use my stick again."
The old woman took a stick from the shop and stirred the solid ghee until it was soft, then filled the pot she had hidden under her shawl.

While she was stealing the ghee her husband allowed the shopkeeper to talk to him and calm him down. When the shopkeeper told the old woman that it was safe to come outside, she was reunited with her husband, and with the ghee safely tucked under her shawl, they set off home.

Once they arrived home they used the ghee to finish making the assidya, ate it and were very happy.

However, when the shopkeeper returned to his shop to serve the next customer, he realised that his ghee had been stolen. A crowd gathered as he ranted and raved trying to work out who had stolen his ghee.
"Did you sell any yesterday?" asked some.
"Did anyone visit your shop?" asked others.
"No, no, no," he replied, "no one except the old couple. I brought the wife into the shop while I tried to calm her husband down."

"Then it must have been them," replied the crowd. "Would you recognize them?"
Everyone helped the shopkeeper search for the old couple, but without success.

Ghubbat Salamah

MUSANDAM GOVERNORATE

Khasab

Bukha

MUSANDAM
GOVERNORATE

Musandam
(Sultanate of Oman)

Daba

Madha

(Sultanate of Oman)

Musandam Governorate

Musandam Governorate the smallest and most northern part of Oman has just 4 wilayats and 31,425 inhabitants. It is separated from the rest of the country by approximately 70 kms of the United Arab Emirates. It is a very important region as this is the gateway to one of the most important shipping lanes in the world, the Straits of Hormuz. It is possibly one of the most dangerous too as Musandam is often called the Norway of Oman because of the wonderful fjords that are unique to this part of the country.

A fjord is a long narrow inlet of water from the sea that has very steep and rugged mountains on both sides. Glaciers caused fjords many thousands of years ago or sometimes they were caused by underwater volcanoes.

Musandam is in fact closer to Iran than it is to the main part of Oman and is believed to have been a haven for pirates and smuggling in the past. Because it is so close to Iran many of the local residents speak a mixture of Arabic and Farsi and local traditions and culture are a blend of both areas. The mountains are very rugged indeed and many rise to over two thousand metres. This means that the lifestyle of the tribes is very harsh and often mountain tribes migrate to the coast to escape the fierce heat of the summer months.

The fjords at Musandam

Musandam has been fought over by the Portuguese and Persians, and in the 19th century the British had a telegraph station in Musandam as part of their link between Bahrain and India. The capital of Musandam is Khasab, once famous for its elegant wooden sailing boats called *battil*. Battils usually have their stern decorated with shells, ribbons and goatskins. Farming and fishing are the major sources of income, though due to improved transport conditions tourism is becoming more popular. Khasab is the Arabic word for fertility and this refers to the very rich soil, fresh water from the mountains and plentiful fishing.

The town of Khasab is a natural harbour, surrounded on three sides by steep mountains. There is a fort which is approximately two hundred and fifty years old and has three cannons facing towards the sea, which were used until very recently to signal the sighting of the moon to indicate the end of Ramadan and the beginning of Eid. In the 16th century the Portuguese had a fort on this site too, probably in recognition of the importance that Musandam held in the region. In the souqs of Musandam you will see lots of Iranian traders who are legal visitors to Oman but are considered smugglers in Iran.

They come from Iran in tiny boats and buy luxury items such as televisions, washing machines, shoes and cigarettes and then sail back to Iran at night hoping that they will not be detected.

Because the area is so mountainous camels are not common in Musandam, but they can be seen in the green meadows around the Rawdah Bowl. Here you will also see Bait Al Qufl, tiny rectangular houses built of local stone and with the roofs made of wood and then covered with earth. Inside the house the floor is one metre below the ground and has raised slabs for sleeping and storing food.

The Bait Al Qufl, which means house of locks, is for the tribes, their flocks and their goods. Each house has two locks to make sure that the house and the goods inside are secure. When the tribes move to the coast in the summer they lock the doors as a sign to everyone else that the house is private, even though it may look deserted.

There is a radar station at Jebal Harem or *mountain of women*, which is the highest mountain in Musandam at 2087 metres. Here it is possible to see wildflowers growing, such as iris and gladioli, not at all what we would expect to see in a desert region.

At Tawi you can observe cave paintings and rock art on the boulders. At Ras Shaykh Masaud you will find the tomb and shrine of an Indian Muslim who died while travelling to Mecca for the Haj. Many Indians consider him a saint and travel to the region to visit his tomb and hope for a blessing.

The origin of the fort at Bukha is disputed. Some say that it was built by the Portuguese, but others say that it was built by Saif Bin Sultan Al Ya'aruby in the early 17th century as he is credited with building so many of the forts in Oman. The fort was restored in 1990 along with many others in the country.

The most northern part of Oman is Kumzar, and as this is the most northern town in Musandam it can only be reached by sea. The Kumzari people speak their own dialect and it is a mixture of Arabic, Farsi, Hindi, Portuguese and English.

FABLE The man who could see water

Long, long ago, everyone in Oman knew Al Sarkhi, the man who could find water. He knew exactly where to find underground water, where to dig wells and make the aflaj. One day the Imam sent for Al Sarkhi and demanded to know about his secret powers. Al Sarkhi replied that if anyone else had asked him about his powers, he would not tell them his secret. However, because the Imam asked, then he must tell his story.

This is Al Sarkhi's story.

When he was a young boy, Al Sarkhi used to hunt in the mountains, plains and wadis. One day while he was hunting, he saw an old man asleep under a tree. Al Sarkhi was quite worried because the man looked tired and sick. Just then the old man woke up, and in a very faint voice, asked Al Sarkhi for a drink of water and some dates.

For three days Al Sarkhi took water and dates to the old man, until he was feeling stronger. The old man was so grateful to Al Sarkhi that on the third day he told him he would like to repay his kindness.

Al Sarkhi did not want anything from the old man, because he thought that he was too old and too poor. Instead, he took him to his village and into his home where he looked after him until he was well again. One day, the old man asked Al Sarkhi to come closer to him. As he moved closer, he felt the old man put some kohl on his eyelids. As soon as Al Sarkhi opened his eyes, he could see everything that was underground, the rocks, water and minerals like copper and gold. Al Sarkhi was so excited that he told the old man what he could see, and immediately the old man put kohl on his eyes again. When he opened his eyes this time Al Sarkhi could still see rocks, water and minerals underground, but not as clearly as before. A third time the old man put kohl on Al Sarkhi's eyes and this time when he opened his eyes, Al Sarkhi could only see water underground.

Al Sarkhi told the old man he could only see water now and the old man replied that this gift, to be able to see water underground would help him and other people. The gift to see gold, copper and rocks would help no one!
So, Al Sarkhi used his gift to help people to find water to bring life to their villages and farms

ASH SHARQIYA REGION
Bawshar
Wadi Al Maawil
Al Amrat
Ar Rustaq
Nakhal
Bidbid
Dama
Wa At Taiyyin
Nizwa
Izki
Manah
Ibra
Wadi Bani
Khalid
Sur
Al Mudaybi
Al Qabil
Adam
Bidiyyah
Al Kamil Wa Al Wafi
Jaalan Bani Bu Hasan
Jaalan Bani Bu Ali
ASH SHARQIYA
REGION
Muhut
Masirah

Ash Sharqiya

Ash Sharqiya, is home to 350,514 people in 11 wilayats. It is an area of contrasts, with mountains, fertile plains and unspoiled beaches. The Hajar Mountains stretch from Ras al Hadd, southeast of Sur, to Musandam in the north. Other well-known features in the Sharqiya region are the vast and isolated Wahiba Sands and Masirah Island, which is well known for its rare shells and turtles. Archaeologists have discovered ancient tombs and settlements at Ibra, Tiwi and Ras Al Junayz that have added historic interest to the region.

Sur is perhaps the best-known town in the Sharqiya region, but there are many other places of interest and things to see. Sur is an ancient port and seafaring town that has strong links to East Africa. When Oman ruled Zanzibar as long ago as the early 19th century, trade goods were imported through Sur. They were sometimes exported to India or sent to the rest of the country. Sur is also one of the most famous towns in Oman for ship building.

The British explorer Tim Severin, who re-created the Sindbad Voyage in 1980, built his dhow *Sohar* in the shipyards of Sur. Traditional boatbuilding skills are still used today. There are no electric drills or rotary saws used. Wooden plugs are used to hold the planks of wood together rather than iron nails, and in the case of Tim Severin's Dhow the planks of wood were actually sewn together with rope - 600 kms to be exact!

Dhows in Sur

Liquified natural gas plant near Sur

With its heritage in ship building it is obvious that a fishing industry is also going to be very important to Sur. The fishermen of Sur were also skilled pearl divers. There is a very interesting maritime museum in Sur for those who are interested in fishing, sailing and boats.

Wood carving is a traditional skill at which Suri men are very skilled. Many of the old houses have wonderfully carved wooden doors with palm trees as the basic design. Music and dance are also key features of the culture and traditions of Sur. As seamen sailed to India and the Far East, they have incorporated many of the music and dance styles that they saw overseas into their local dances, making them very interesting and different to other regions in Oman.

Advances in technology have found a home in Sur also. The Oman LNG - Liquefied Natural Gas plant was built in 1999 just north of the town centre. Three hundred and sixty kilometers of pipeline carry dry gas from central Oman to Sur for the liquefication process. The first successful shipment was sent to South Korea. Further development has emerged in the region as the Oman India Fertilizer Company is building a plant just south of the Oman LNG plant.

A 170 mts long and 10 mts wide suspension bridge, the first of its kind in Oman has been built over the creek in Sur linking Al Aijah and Khor al Batah and saving 10 kms travel between the two. The bridge was officallly opened in 2010.

The village of Akhdar, not far from Sur, has very skilled weavers; shawls, bed covers and wall hangings are made using the traditional purple, blue, silver and yellow threads. One of the weavers is reputed to make the material from which His Majesty Sultan Qaboos turbans are made.

In Sinaw, in the local souq, women work alongside the men selling their goods. Many of them can be seen wearing the traditional mask called a burka. This mask covers the whole face and is made from shiny metallic fabric.

The old town of Sinaw has two walled villages and one of the last remaining falaj clocks that is still in working condition. The clock is used to indicate when water can be allowed to pass through the falaj to different parts of the village.

Ibra is the gateway to the Sharqiya region as you travel from Muscat to Sur. There are many watchtowers in the area so this is always an indication of just how important this town was in the past. Many forts and fortified houses make a visit to Ibra very interesting.

There are some very interesting mosques in Ibra, both old and new. There is an old sacrificial mosque where holy men, who were often hermits, gave blessing to the local village people. It is still used today for sacrifices and offerings of clothing, food and sometimes animals are left in the mountains.

The Wednesday morning souq in Ibra is the place to be! However, only if you are a woman! It is the only souq in Oman that is for women only! The women sell goods that they have made or goods that women like to buy – dress materials, perfume, fruit and vegetables, carpets and make-up, and at the same time they exchange the local news and items of interest.

The Wahiba Sands is the traditional home of the Bedouin tribes. Most of the desert in Oman is rocky and gravel covered, but in the Wahiba Sands, there are rolling sand dunes of every colour from gold to deep red. The Wahiba Sands covers an area of a hundred and eighty kms from north to south and eighty kms from east to west. That is a lot of sand and a lot of space to get lost in, especially when the jinns or sand devils blow! These whirlwinds whip up the sand into funnels and race along the surface.

Some of the sand dunes can reach 100 metres high. That makes them as tall as some mountains so it is very easy to get lost.

The eastern side of the dunes has large forest areas and so provides shelter and a refuge for the Bedouin, plants and wildlife.

On the coastal side of Sharqiya, there are lots of places of interest, but perhaps the most famous are Ras al Hadd and Ras Al Junayz. These two areas are well known for their turtle nesting grounds, and each year thousands of turtles come to these beaches to lay their eggs. All the turtles will have been born on these same beaches thirty years ago and will continue to come to these beaches to lay their eggs.

The eggs are buried in the sand and when it is time for the hatchlings to make their way to the sea, sadly only a very small percentage will survive. Each turtle will lay up to one hundred eggs but only approximately twenty will survive. Seagulls, crabs and foxes will have eaten those that do not.

Masirah Island is eighteen kms wide and sixty kms in length. It is windswept and barren, and has a very small population. However it is very famous for its rare seashells and nesting sites of loggerhead turtles.

FABLE Burooj Kibaykib

Al Jayalah Tombs

In the Sharqiya region, near Ibra, legend tells us there was once a tyrant called Kibaykib who built two towers, because he wanted to live in them both. Everyone said that Kibaykib had a magic sword that could cut rocks into two pieces.

A Bedouin called Qadah, asked a jinn at the spring of Ayn Naghb to help him to kill Kibaykib. This is the plan that the jinn made.

The jinn told the Bedouin to find Kibaykib lying down with his eyes closed, which mant he was awake, but if he had his eyes open then he was asleep. If Kibaykib was asleep then the magic sword could be taken from him.

The jinn told Qadah where to find Kibaykib so Qadah took some friends and went in search of him.

They soon found Kibaykib and saw that his eyes were open, which meant that he was asleep, so they crept up to him and took away his sword. However, before they could use the sword to kill him, Kibaykib woke up, saw Qadah and his friends and ran away and hid in a cave.

Qadah and his friends eventually found Kibaykib and struck him with the magic sword cutting him into two halves. Kibaykib's head and shoulders fell to the ground, but his legs and lower body ran a long way before they too fell to the ground, dead.

That is why Kibaykib needed two tomb towers, both called Qabor Kibaykib but some distance apart, one for his head and shoulders and the other for his legs.

FABLE Majlis al Jinn

My grandfather told me this story, and his grandfather told him, and his grandfather told him – so it must be true. Many, many years ago, a Bedouin left her goats and went to get some food. She thought the goats were safe because they were inside an enclosure. When she returned she found a leopard guarding seven baby goats that it had killed.

The woman was very upset and angry so she took her axe and tried to kill the leopard. As she lifted the axe the leopard swiped her body with one of his great paws and blinded her with the other paw. Determined to kill the leopard the woman split the leopard's head in two with the axe as she fell to the ground and died. The woman's family found her and the leopard dead in each other's arms. In honour of her bravery, God made seven stars fall from the sky, which created the seven sinkholes or khoshilat. The largest of these is known as Majlis al Jinn or Khoshilat Maqandeli.

FABLE The house of gold

At Tiwi in the Sharqiya region, there is a very special house - or at least the remains of the house.

High, high on a hill above Tiwi there was once a very majestic-looking house owned by Ibn Mukarab from eastern Saudi Arabia.

Ibn Mukarab was a poet and a very rich man, but he had made some enemies in his home town so he decided to run away and hide in Tiwi where he built his mansion. He decided to build his house high on a hill so that he could see if his enemies were chasing him and also see who was coming to visit him.

Before he died, Ibn Mukarab had made arrangements for his body to be buried in a cave on a hill on the opposite side of the wadi. He had arranged for steps to be built up to the cave where he wanted his body to be placed.

He was a very cunning man and had a carefully arranged plan. As the steps were built up the hillside to the cave, he put gold under each step.

Now you probably think that was a very silly thing to do? But, Ibn Mukarab's plan was very clever indeed.

By putting gold under the steps, he knew that once he was buried, people would break the steps to get to the gold. The steps would therefore be destroyed and his enemies would never be able to reach him.

GOVERNORATE OF AL BURAIMI
Mahadah
United Arab Emirates
Al Buraymi
As Sunaynah
Dank

Al Buraimi

Previously part of the Ad Dhahirah region, Buraimi the newest of the Governorates was created by Royal decree in October 2006. Buraimi's importance stems from its strategic location in the north- west of the Sultanate and at Wadi Jissi has one of the main border posts for entrance into the United Arab Emirates at Al Ain. It is therefore an important trade route. Buraimi is an oasis town and has an abundant water supply due to its wadis and falaj systems and therefore is able to produce wheat, dates and fruits.

Buraimi has a population of 72,917

Fossil valley found to the East of the Buraimi Township contains many fossilised remains of prehistoric creatures. Buraimi, the place where Islam first entered Oman and the crossroad between the Arabian Peninsula and the coast of Oman, is a historical and prosperous town. There are lots of watchtowers and forts, which indicate that in the past there has been the need to guard the area carefully, but today it is a peaceful border town. However just fifty years ago in 1952 Saudi Arabia decided that they owned Buraimi and moved in! Three years later they were driven out and both sides now agree that Buraimi is one hundred percent Omani.

AL WUSTA REGION

Al Wusta

Al Wusta is the second largest of the regions in Oman, at least in terms of the area that it covers, but it is has one of the smallest population only 42,111.

Most of the region is desert, but it has the oldest rocks in Oman at Duqm and Nafun. On the coastal plains and in the lagoons there are gazelles, oryx, flamingoes, turtles, dolphins and shells. On the island of Mahout, which is the northern border, there are forests of black mangrove and lots of prawns.

Most of Oman's oil comes from the 600,000,000 year old rocks of the Al Huqf group. Commercially it is some of the oldest oil in the world.

At Duqm the main industry is fishing, and in the hills camel breeding. The women spin and weave cloth from goat's wool, or make baskets from skin and leaves.

The Jiddat Al Harasis is part of a nature reserve that has been set up to re-establish the herds of the Arabian Oryx (or White Oryx) that had previously been hunted close to extinction. Wadi Yalooni is the actual project base, and thanks to the dedication and action of His Majesty Sultan Qaboos, Oryx that had been bred in San Diego zoo have now been released into the wild and are at home in the Jiddat Al Harasis. The men of the Harasis tribe have become rangers, dedicated to protecting the Oryx.

There are many small, interesting villages in the area, with names that are not as well known as those of the other regions. This is because tourism and even local visitors are not common. Ras Madrakah has white sandy beaches and black volcanic rocks. This is an ideal place to see turtles, and dolphins.

Some of the caves have wooden doors indicating they have been used by the fishermen to store their catch and valuables. At Khawr, there is a waterhole where you can see camels and gazelles grazing, while flamingoes and herons look for food in the shallow waters. In Sawqirah bay in 1763 a ship called the Amstelveen was sunk. Seventy people died and the thirty-five survivors decided to walk to Muscat, at the time the nearest point of civilization, but only eight people actually arrived in Muscat.

At Wadi Shuwaymiyah the limestone gorge has been carved into wonderful shapes and patterns by the weather. A freshwater pool with palm trees and shrubs creates a tropical effect. The gorge is a haven for ibex, hyena and gazelles. Fossils that have been found in the gorge tell us that the sea once covered the area.

FABLE Dancing with fire

Once upon a time in the Al Wusta region of Oman there was a woman called Shaifirah from the village of Shuwaymiyah. Shaifirah was a member of the Batahira tribe and was known in the whole region for the dancing skills that she had inherited from her mother. Shaifirah was particularly good at the dance known as *naash* where the women move and swing their long hair in rhythm to the beat of the music. One day, the women and dancers of Shuwaymiyah were invited to a wedding of the tribe of the Harasis. Now, the dancers of the Harasis and the dancers of Shuwaymiyah were rivals and very soon the dancing became a competition to prove how was best. As the evening wore on it became clear that the daughter of Budaith from the Harsusi tribe was the best dancer. The dancers from the Shuwaymiyah could not believe that they were not the best dancers, so they called Shaifirah to dance for them.

Shaifirah said that she could not dance because she had had a baby girl three days before and her figure was not as good as it used to be. She had also decided that it was time for her to retire from dancing. Shaifirah's sisters had other ideas! They decided that Shaifirah must dance; it was her duty to dance, to save the tribe's reputation as well as her moral obligation. Of course, Shaifirah had no choice - she had to dance. She put on her dancing costume and rode her camel towards the contest, which originally began as a wedding!

Shaifirah was determined to win the contest, so she asked her friends to bring her some wood that they had lit in the fire. With the burning wood wrapped around her hair, Shaifirah entered the dancing circle. She began to sway and dance as never before. She was quickly surrounded by the women of both tribes who stood in silence, stunned by her beauty and in awe of her dancing skills. The crowd was mesmerized with her joyous and fiery dance.

As Shaifirah fell to the ground unconscious, she was crowned the most talented dancer in the region.

Delighted and proud to be crowned the best dancer in the region Shaifirah returned home to her baby daughter and lived happily ever after.